MW01706246

Portable Selling

James S. Scherrer

and

Peter G. Randall

Brady Publishing

New York London Toronto Sydney Tokyo Singapore

Copyright © 1992 by James S. Scherrer and Peter G. Randall
All rights reserved, including the right of reproduction
in whole or in part in any form.

Brady Publishing

A Division of Prentice Hall Computer Publishing
15 Columbus Circle
New York, NY 10023

Manufactured in the United States of America

10 9 8 7 6 5 4 3 2 1

ISBN 1-56686-019-9

Credits

Publisher
Michael Violano

Managing Editor
Kelly D. Dobbs

Editor
Susan Hunt

Production Editor
Tom Dillon

Copy Editors
William Kriegsman
Cynthia Lamb

Book Designer
Scott Cook

Cover Designer
HUB Graphics

Production Team
Katy Bodenmiller
Lisa Daugherty
John Kane
Sean Medlock
Roger Morgan
Juli Pavey
Linda Quigley
Michelle Self
Susan Shepard
Greg Simsic
Marcella Thompson
Angie Trzepacz

Limits of Liability and Disclaimer of Warranty

The authors and publisher of this book have used their best efforts in preparing this book and the programs contained in it. These efforts include the research and testing of these programs to determine their effectiveness. The authors and publisher make no warranty of any kind, expressed or implied, with regard to these programs or the documentation contained in this book. The authors and publisher shall not be liable in any event for incidental or consequential damages in connection with, or arising out of, the furnishing, performance, or use of these programs.

Trademarks

Most computer and software brand names have trademarks or registered trademarks. The individual trademarks have not been listed here.

Acknowledgments

We would like to thank the efforts of our editing team at Brady Publishing: Susan Hunt, Tom Dillon, Bill Kriegsman, and Kelly Dobbs.

Contents

Introduction

This book is about empowering field sales representatives with the latest in computing technology. All manner of other professionals have been empowered, and now is the time to outfit the "computerized field sales person." The infantry has its guns; the paratroopers their parachutes; the secretaries their word processors. Now it's time for the most important part of corporate America—the revenue-generating sales professionals—to get their tools.

It has been said that nothing happens until a sale is made . . . and we agree. This book is filled with ideas about how to generate more sales in shorter time periods, and with greater profit potential. In short, this book is about supercharging the field salesperson—literally injecting them with adrenaline—for maximum sales performance.

If Willy Loman—the fictional traveling salesman of Arthur Miller's play, *Death of a Salesman*—had a PC, would he have enjoyed a more successful career?

Technology cannot transform you into a super salesperson—you need to have sales in your blood—but a PC can help you work more efficiently, contact more people, maintain better schedules, stay on target, and never miss a follow up. These attributes make the PC an indispensable tool for the modern salesperson.

"How can a PC help me?" you might ask. "Other than spreadsheets and word processors for creating sales plans, and desktop publishing programs for generating sales literature, what else can I do with a PC?"

You can use the following:

- Personal Information Managers (PIMs) to manage your time. PIMs will alert you when it is time to head out for meetings, make initial and follow-up telephone calls, and organize your life. No more notes scrawled on scraps of paper, napkins, and the backs of envelopes.
- Graphing programs to monitor and track your progress
- Project scheduling software will ensure that your sales plans happen on target
- Telecommunication software to relay information from the field to the home office
- On-line databases and CD ROMs to create prospect lists containing highly qualified leads
- Fax boards and integrated telecommunications products to launch cost-effective direct-mail campaigns
- Integrated sales contact software that will organize your entire office and sales efforts
- Sales presentation tools to dazzle your clients
- Quote development tools that will allow you to create customized quotes at the push of a button
- Telemarketing software that will send your message out to prospective clients at astonishing speeds

Portable Selling is divided into three sections that will explain how current software and hardware products allow you to do all of the preceding and more. Section I is designed to show you the many options available for portable computers in the market today. It focuses on the key areas in which PCs and laptops can improve your sales effectiveness. You'll find plenty of dos and don'ts, as well as references to specific vendors. The goal of this section is not to explain which keys you need to press to make an electronic diary entry or tap into an on-line database, but how electronic diaries can help you plan your meetings and callbacks and how you can quickly and inexpensively collect valuable sales leads.

Section II presents case studies of sales people who have put their computers to good use and, as a result, enjoy higher sales levels, higher efficiency, and less hectic lives. The scenarios include the following:

- An integrated sales support software system
- An integrated financial client support system
- A computerized real estate sales and prospecting system
- Use of portable computers in sales presentations
- A database marketing project

The third section is an introduction to the Sales Ally software provided with this book. This program, with a retail value of $395, has received the PC Magazine's Editors' Choice award. Sales Ally is a complete system for managing contacts, including the following:

- Record file—name, address, phone number, etc.
- User-defined fields
- Prospect and customer tracking
- Unlimited contacts per company
- Notepad of conversations
- Quik Letter and proposals
- Tickler file and calling lists
- Autodialing with a modem
- Calling statistics
- Automatic lead loading capability from a floppy disk
- Word processing with Mail Merge
- WordPerfect and Word compatibility
- Cross-referencing

- Order entry system
- Sales forecasting
- Invoicing
- ASCII data transferring
- Importing and exporting with duplicate record considerations
- Context-sensitive Help
- Pop-up calculator, calendar, and alert reminder
- Scratch pad
- Scripting
- Hot keys to other programs
- Macros
- Multiple database management
- ID/password system

By reading this book and then putting the Sales Ally to work in your office, you'll find yourself working more efficiently and in total command of your prospects and customer base.

■ ■ ■

The old way of doing sales, Willy Loman style, is nearing death. Good! We say good-bye to the traditional approach and welcome the new, "fully powered" traveling salesperson of the 90s. You will discover in this book that unparalleled sales success is just a few keystrokes away.

Jim Scherrer
Peter G. Randall
Philadelphia, PA

July, 1992

1

Finding Sales Leads Part I: Paper Sources

Leads are the life blood of the salesperson, and there are many ways that the computer can help you manage the lead-development process. In this chapter, we will consider how you can use your computer to maintain a database of leads obtained from directories, purchased lists, and other print sources.

Paper Sources

While not as "sexy" as electronic sources, which we will discuss in the next chapter, printed directories and mailing lists still constitute the bulk of the currently available list data. Perhaps in the not-to-distant future, everything you want will have an electronic and paper equivalent, but for now, many lead sources are still in paper-only format. First, we'll explain where to look for leads; then, we will discuss how the computer fits into the picture.

Phone Directories

These might seem obvious, but they're often overlooked. If you work locally, phone directories are crucial. If you are national in scope, a good library will have current phone directories for all the major U.S. cities, or you can obtain them from the local telephone companies for a nominal charge. Don't forget, many companies have converted to toll-free numbers as their primary access, so be sure to get the *AT&T Toll-Free 800 Business Directory* as well. Beyond the familiar yellow pages put out by the local telephone companies, you can get competing directories such as the *Donnelly Directory*.

Newspapers

Read the newspapers with an eye towards prospects. Stories often contain company names. Ads for products and services, as well as employment ads and classifieds can also be a gold mine. Best of all, you can research leads while sipping your morning coffee!

Trade Magazines

Most trade associations have publications that cover current industry news, who's who, new products, etc. Business libraries carry trade magazines, and you can get subscriptions through the associations. Scan every page for names and companies and add them to your prospect list. You can often buy the magazine's mailing list on a price per name basis usually ranging from 50 cents to 85 cents a name, although the cost can be much higher for specialized lists or pre-qualified lists.

Major Business Publications

Do the same as with the trade magazines. If you sell to the electronics world, then whenever you read about a company that has embarked on an electronics venture, capture the name. Again, consider purchasing the publication's mailing list. They can and will sell a subset based on geographic area or other appropriate selection criteria.

Association Lists

For every profession or industry, you'll find at least one trade association. Check in the *Encyclopedia of Associations and National Organizations of the U.S.* published by Gale Research, Inc. (which you can also access on-line). Each association has different policies regarding its lists. In some cases, you may have to join the organization and will then be entitled to a membership directory. In other cases, you may be able to purchase the list or directory. Either way, a trade association can be an excellent source of current data for your field.

Specialized Newsletters

Check *Ulrich's International Periodicals Directory* (published by R.R. Bowker), which lists thousands of magazines and newsletters. Write or call the publishers and ask for samples in your field. You might decide that some of the publications are worth spending the money for a regular subscription.

Government Sources

State and federal Departments of Commerce can provide a wealth of data about companies in your area. Be sure to check with your local Chamber of Commerce, too.

Commercial Lists

There are innumerable lists available from commercial list brokers throughout the world. You can find list brokers that specialize in everything from plumbers to pilots. The hardest part of using a list broker is finding the right list for your product. One place you might begin is a publication called the *Directory of Mailing List Companies* published by Todd Publications. This directory lists more than 1,000 list brokers and managers who control more than 25,000 different lists. The broker is listed alphabetically and then cross-referenced by category. Again, you will need to create your list-development strategy before you become overwhelmed with names and addresses. Unless your product truly requires a shotgun approach, you will be far better off executing with precision, not volume. After you have picked a list, you can request a sub-set of the total list based on geography or some other criteria.

Converting the Data

When you have leads from these sources, what will you do with them? You can stack them on your desk or pile them onto the front seat of your car. Both are highly inefficient in terms of weeding out redundancies and maintaining follow-up lists. A better way is to organize the data on your computer. Although this means that you have to input the information, it's well worth the effort. After you've captured the data, you can create reports that will enable you to carry out methodical contact and follow-up actions, generate mailing labels, and track your results.

Choosing a Computer Program

You will want to maintain your lead information in some kind of database, which means that you have a wide variety of software options. The choice of a database really comes down to your programming skills and how much "horsepower" you're toting around on your laptop. You basically have three choices when it comes to list management software:

1. low-cost, simple databases
2. high-cost, full-feature databases
3. specialty list-management packages

A Note about Power

Of all the criteria in choosing a database program, the power of your computer is the easiest to evaluate. First, you must determine the amount of RAM your machine contains, the size of hard disk (if it has one), and its available space. Then you can determine—from a particular software package's minimum system requirements—whether you have enough "horsepower" to run the program. For example, dBASE IV requires 3.5 megabytes of hard disk space for just the program, before you load any data. If you don't have a hard disk or if you don't have at least 3.5 megabytes of available space, don't consider dBASE IV without factoring in the cost of upgrading your system.

HARDWARE HINT

While there are tremendous "bargains" available for 286 and prior chip-based computers, you will save yourself money in the long run with at least a 386 SX based PC. Not only will you get better performance, but there is already software on the market that *requires* a 386 processor, and that number will continue to grow. Some computer users refer to the 286 chip as being "brain dead." We won't go that far, but we do believe that it is dead in the market place.

If you have not yet purchased your computer, you need to ensure that you purchase enough hardware to run your selected software. Every software package will supply the minimum requirements, but you should look beyond those minimum requirements to the reasonable performance requirements. If you are in doubt, call the software company's customer service department, or preferably, their technical support line and ask for advice. Also, when choosing a computer, think about allowing room for future growth.

Programming

As for programming, you can purchase many general-purpose databases that require no formal training, such as *My Database* or *X* or *Y*. Be aware that while the extremely simple low-end database programs have a quick learning curve and low cost ($0 for shareware and up to $100 for simple commercial packages), they also have extreme limitations, and you may quickly outgrow them.

On the other end of the spectrum, software packages such as dBASE IV, Paradox, and RBASE have steep learning curves and may require many hours, days, or weeks to develop fully functioning databases if you've never done so before. You might be able to find someone in your company who can create a database for you using one of the high-end programs, or if you don't know an experienced database user, you could hire a programmer to write a custom lead database tailored to your needs.

You will find many fine programs, such as Alpha 4, at the mid-range level. These databases require no formal training, but a higher-than-novice level of knowledge with computers is needed. As you become more proficient with these programs, you'll find many built-in capabilities that enable you to create sophisticated databases. In short, this is a range of programs that can grow with you.

Finally, if you're familiar with Lotus 1-2-3 or Excel, or even your word-processing program, you might consider using their built-in database functions. Although the databases found in spreadsheets and word processors are not as versatile as dedicated database programs, they may be fine for your lead management needs. An

.ıvantage to spreadsheet or word processor databases is if you are comfortable with them, you can focus on making sales calls rather than pressing keys.

Non-Programming Databases and Specialty List Programs

If you are not a programmer and do not wish to become one, don't despair. Many salesmen before you have developed their own solutions and—Surprise! Surprise!—they are willing to sell them to you. Many of these custom sales and list management programs are, frankly, garbage. Created by individual sales reps for their personal needs, these programs are later packaged for sale because there might be a chance to make a buck. The author may be a great salesman, but he probably isn't a great programmer. More importantly, there usually isn't a significant company to backup the product for future development and support. Fortunately, there are several exceptions.

Label Printing Software

Most sales lists are used to print labels for direct mail campaigns. If this is your only objective, you should look at two very inexpensive ($50–$70) label printing programs that are published by—you guessed it—the label manufacturers. LablePro is published by Avery and Laser-Ready Labels is published by 3M. As their names imply, you will get better results with a laser printer, but you can also use a high-resolution dot-matrix or ink jet printer. Of these two programs, we prefer the Avery product for flexibility and ease of use. Both allow you to create databases and import data from a variety of formats. All label formats of the publisher are supported and a wide variety of fonts and layouts can be produced. Even suitable graphics are included. The only real limitation is that these programs only work with labels—there are no mailmerge or follow-up capabilities.

Sales Automation Software

As you might have guessed, the sales automation software that is the focus of the second and third sections of this book can really do it all. One of the more basic functions is the capability of printing mailing labels and creating mailmerge documents. Although the label printing software supports a wider variety of labels and formats, the label printing functions of the integrated packages can get the basic job done. In addition, these programs provide the capability to perform automated follow up on the initial mailing, as well as manage the customers that eventually choose to purchase your product. Two of the most highly regarded of these products are Sales Ally and ACT! Although Sales Ally offers more sales support and sales management functions, both have sophisticated list management capabilities that can create, import, and subset data on a wide range of criteria. They retail in various forms from $200 to $800.

NOTE

Please note that a completely operational copy of Sales Ally 3.1 is contained in the back of this book. You are free to use this copy as you chose within the limits of the licensing agreement. You can contact Sales Ally at (215) 836-1830 for further information about purchasing a complete user manual and obtaining current versions of the software.

Entering Data

Essentially, you have three ways to get data into your computer: manually enter it; buy it on disk in a compatible or ASCII format; or scan it.

Manual Data Entry

The main considerations involved with manual entry are time, cost, and accuracy. Your efforts to locate leads and set up a database can be undermined by clerical sloppiness and inevitable typographical errors. This is especially important if your first contact will be by mail—no one likes to have their name misspelled. Therefore, make sure that proofreading is part of the process. For this type of data entry, it's best to have two people proof the work. One person reads the information from the paper source, but the other checks the entry on screen. It's tedious, but foolproof. Besides, if it's worth entering, it's worth proofing.

Before you invest the time and money to manually keypunch data, invest a dime in a phone call. Many organizations are more than willing to provide publicly available data on a disk at a nominal charge.

Compatible Disk Formats/ASCII

You can often purchase information in popular database formats that enable you to simply import the data into your selected software. Also, you may be able to purchase data in a generic ASCII format. Virtually every software program allows you to import data in ASCII form. Your software manual should explain how to import ASCII data into the program. If you have commissioned a custom database, be sure that your programmer includes a menu option for handling ASCII file imports.

If you are importing data into a database (as opposed to a word processor) you should ensure that it is in Comma Delimited ASCII form. This just means that each field of text is surrounded by quotes and that each field (both text and number) is separated from the next by a comma. This format makes the process of placing the correct data in the proper field much easier for the importing program.

Scanning

One of the most exciting options for scanners is Optical Character Recognition or OCR. With OCR, you place your document on a scanner (such as a Hewlett-Packard ScanJet), the scanner reads the print, and the software enters data into your computer. Sounds great, doesn't it? Unfortunately, it can be very problematic. Accuracy is the main issue; although OCR programs improve all the time, you must still carefully check every entry. A lot depends on the quality, size, and style of the source document's type. If you receive a fax and then scan it, chances are, you'll get numerous errors. Even under the best circumstances, no one can guarantee 100-percent accuracy. Also, be aware that when you scan in data you will create an ASCII file and will still have to import it into your database.

One interesting breakthrough with OCR has been pioneered by Caere in its OmniPage Direct program ($300–$600). OmniPage Direct can scan data directly into the specific format of the target application program, such as word processors, databases, spreadsheets, etc. In another version of OmniPage, Caere worked directly with Hewlett-Packard in the development of their HP ScanJet IIc scanner and Omnipage Professional software. These two products have a special hardware-software link that, when working together, allows them to produce extraordinary accuracy with less than perfect originals. If you plan to do a lot of scanning, you must look into this combination. Beware however, such power does have its costs. The scanner retails for more than $2,000, and the OmniPage Professional software alone costs $1,000. In addition, you will need at least a 386 processor with 4 megabytes of RAM and a large hard disk (100 megabytes or better is advised).

Many hand-held scanners are supported by OCR packages. In fact, it is *extremely* difficult to accurately scan in directories or lists by hand, and you might find yourself in a frustrating situation with little usable data to show for your effort.

Fax Scanning

A new twist on OCR involves software that uses internal fax boards. Software such as FaxGrabber and Intel's FAXability Plus/OCR enable you to receive a fax and then convert the fax into a format that you can edit. (Without the OCR capability, you can only read or print an inbound fax.) Again, accuracy is a concern. It's not perfect, but it is worth considering.

…nside Advice

- *Look under your nose.* Some of the best lead sources are available without much digging—in magazines, local associations, Rotary Clubs, chambers of commerce, etc.

- *Tailor a database to your needs.* If you just want a list of numbers that weeds out duplicates, provides a means to check off calls, and indicates when call backs should be made, keep your database simple. Use a program with which you are familiar—your spreadsheet or word processor may do. If you want a sophisticated lead tracking system, try a specialty sales automation system—like Sales Ally—rather than spending hours of valuable prospecting time developing a custom system yourself.

- *Use scanning with optimistic caution.* View it as a tool with potential flaws. Remember, carefully check all manually entered data. Just entering data into your system is not enough—you need accurate data in terms of names, addresses, telephone and fax numbers. One wrong digit or letter, and you've wasted your effort. On the other hand, every correct entry means a potential sale!

- *Quality over Quantity.* There is a not too ancient proverb about a drunk looking under the street lamp for his car keys, because the light was better. The same idea applies to mailing lists. Don't fall for the temptation to use an inferior list because it is cheap or conveniently available on disk. Likewise, don't be tempted to use a larger list just because of its size—you may end up spending more money on mailing costs and receiving an inferior list.

  A quality list has two key features: First, it is deliverable, meaning that when you mail the letter it gets to the person. (A 98% deliverable list is okay, 100% is fantastic). Second, it is a list of actively interested buyers, who are direct mail responsive (remember that many people discard mail before opening).

- *Qualify before you buy.* Figure out how you are going to qualify a list before you buy it (either by purchasing it or investing the time to obtain and enter it). Better yet, consider purchasing a pre-qualified list. Be sure to evaluate the process of pre-qualifying.

- *Test before you invest.* Many list brokers will allow you to test a list before you buy it (for a price). Try out a large list by sending a test sample to 5 or 10 percent of the total list. If the test is successful, you can follow up with the remainder. Even if you already own the entire list, sample it before you invest in a major mailing.

■ ■ ■

Finding Sales Leads Part II: Electronic Sources

In Chapter 1, we discussed the importance of paper sources—directories, lists, etc.—and how to enter them efficiently into your computer. Here, the focus is on important electronic sources of sales lead information: electronic databases, floppy-based information sources, and CD-ROM. For the traveling road warrior, electronic sources are just a modem call or disk read away.

Electronic Databases

In the coming age of information, everything that exists in print form will have a digital counterpart. Although that day has yet to arrive, more and more important information is now accessible through on-line databases that offer a wealth of bibliographic citations, abstracts, and full-text articles. Some databases even offer the electronic equivalent of the "yellow pages," containing thousands of business names and addresses. These sources can be found on information powerhouses such as Dialog, from Dialog Information Services and BRS, managed by BRS Information Services. Dow Jones offers extensive company and business information through the Dow Jones News Retrieval service. In addition, information utilities such as CompuServe offer extensive searching capabilities that allow you to scan vast amounts of data with just a few keystrokes.

…o access an electronic database, you must first sign up. This process generally requires credit card information for billing and a little bit of paperwork. Some systems will enroll you over the phone, then send confirming paperwork. Either way, it's easy. Next, you will need to purchase a modem and communications software if you don't already own them. Many of the more popular databases and information services will sell their own communication programs for a modest fee. These dedicated packages make it easy to log on, find your way around the menus and commands, and capture information. The disadvantage is that you can't use these programs to log on to other databases or for general communications with other parties.

After you're set up, dial into a local access number and connect with the database. You will then log on by typing your account and password information. When you set up the software, you'll be prompted to enter all key numbers. With a general communications package, you will have to follow the instructions for each database and type in the required information as codes. Full-feature packages like Crosstalk MK4 and Crosstalk for Windows allow you to write scripts for logging on. For example, if you are using Crosstalk, set the program for "learn" mode, log on, and the software will remember your keystrokes. If you link the script to the phone number, the next time you call the database Crosstalk will "know" to send your accounting and password information when prompted.

However you choose to log on to an electronic database to locate and retrieve sales leads, bear in mind the following cautions:

1. *Know your goals.* The worst time to use an electronic database is when you don't know exactly what you want. Probing an on-line database is not like thumbing through stacks of library books—every moment you spend browsing costs money.

2. *It's important to develop a search strategy before logging on.* Information is costly; the more you plan your session while you're on-line, the more the session will cost you. For example, if you're going to access a database of recent business literature for leads, list the criteria for your search. Do you only

want articles within the past six months? Do you want to limit your search to the U.S.? It is better to answer these questions ahead of time than after retrieving hundreds of useless records, each with a price tag.

The most important command to learn with any database, next to logging on, is logging off!

---

3. *Make "guerrilla" attacks on the database.* Rather than logging on and gathering as much information as possible, make small forays into the database. This way, if your information search strategy is yielding less-than-useful information, you can change your approach and cut your losses.
4. *Capture data and print it later.* Never print out data screen by screen while you are paying for connect time. Use your software package's capture program; then print out the data when you're off-line.

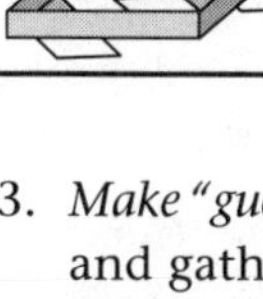

Most databases allow you to access data at 300, 1200, or 2400 baud and charge a higher premium for the faster speeds. The speed you choose will depend on what you intend to do while on-line. If you are typing in queries, but not downloading a lot of information, you may save money by selecting a lower speed. No one we know can out-type 300 baud. If, on the other hand, you are downloading a large file of names, it is often cheaper to choose a higher speed. The small additional charge for the higher speed is offset by the reduction in time spent on-line.

All of the major telecommunication companies used to access on-line databases—Tymenet, Sprintnet, Dialnet—have different local phone numbers for different cities. Before you travel, ask for a booklet or download a listing of those numbers.

Disk-Based Information Systems

A wealth of sales lead information can be obtained in disk and CD-ROM format. For example, many mailing lists are available on disk. Some companies—such as General Information, publisher of Hotline—offer extensive electronic phone books in general business categories as well as specialized areas. You can browse through the phone books and create your own custom lists. Another source is OnDisk Information Systems, which offers a database on disk that contains more than 160,000 computer hardware and software manufacturers.

What can you do with disk-based information? That depends on the data on the disks. With OnDisk databases, you can select companies on the basis of industry importance, financial status, product type, etc. and then generate customized mailing lists tailored to your needs.

CD-ROM Disks

CD-ROM (read-only memory) is an optical technology that enables information suppliers to cram large amounts of information on a single optical disk using similar technology to music CDs. The advantages, from an information density standpoint, are clear: one CD-ROM can hold the data contained in hundreds of phone books. Lists on Disk by the Optical Products Division of American Business Information ($750 base subscription) contains more than 9 million business names and addresses. You can select companies by geographical area, SIC code, and many other considerations and only pay for the data you select.

So why not do away with floppies? Or hard disks for that matter? Unfortunately, CD-ROMs are slow—even slower than floppy drives. Whereas a fast hard disk can find any piece of data in about 12 milliseconds, even a fast CD-ROM drive (for instance, the NEC Intersect drive) has an access time of more than 300 milliseconds. Three hundred milliseconds may seem fast, but remember that it is 25 times slower than a fast hard disk. So, until that access time is greatly reduced, there will be a thriving business in floppies and hard disks despite the enormous storage capacity of their optical counterparts. CD-ROM also is read-only. You cannot add to or change the data on a CD-ROM.

Connecting a CD-ROM Drive

Most CD-ROM drives connect to your computer by a special port called SCSI (pronounced scuzzy). On a desktop system, you can generally plug a SCSI card into an available expansion slot and connect the drive to the SCSI board. Install the software by following the installation routine, and your computer will recognize the CD-ROM drive as the next logical drive. So, if your hard disk is your *C* drive, your CD-ROM will become your *D* drive.

Because most portable computers do not have expansion board capabilities, you may need a special connector. The key consideration for the mobile salesperson is the weight and mass of the drive. An external CD-ROM drive can weigh two to three times as much as your computer and occupy twice the space. NEC and several other manufacturers offer very small, portable CD-ROM drives slightly larger than portable music CD players. These smaller versions will serve you better on the road.

The Multimedia Connection

One final factor to consider when purchasing a CD-ROM drive is whether or not it conforms to the MPC multimedia standard. If it does, you will be able to purchase disks that do a marvelous job of integrating visual images and sounds, which can be played through stereo speakers or headsets. Many drives can play music CDs as well. Although this will not make any difference for preparing cold call and prospect lists, your children and family can enjoy the ability to use exciting educational and recreational disks. Besides, after a long day on the road, you probably wouldn't mind a multimedia adventure game yourself.

Inside Advice

- *On-line information may be powerful, but it often comes at a price.* The key to getting good sales lead and prospect information from an electronic database is to cut your on-line time to a minimum. On a per minute basis, the charges may not seem outrageous, but as the minutes tick away, it is easy to rack up a large bill.

- *Qualify your leads when using disk-based information.* Even though you have purchased the disks and own the information (as long as you don't turn around and sell it verbatim in the exact form of the disk—that would violate copyright), don't go "hog wild." Simply because you have 9 million names at your disposal does not mean that you should mail to all of them (quick—how much is 9 million multiplied by 29 cents: the price of first-class stamps). Qualify your leads carefully by selecting the most important criteria. Otherwise, you'll be wasting your time, energy, and money.

■ ■ ■

3

Making the First Contact

In Chapters 1 and 2, we discussed opportunities for using your computer to gain valuable leads. In this chapter, we'll discuss techniques for putting those leads to good use. First, though, we need to touch on the issue of lead qualification. You probably know from experience the frustration of wasting your time on leads that go nowhere. Unfortunately, a danger of prospecting in the Electronic Age is finding yourself deluged with potential leads. Only a fraction of these will be useful. Therefore, apply the tightest possible "filters" when downloading information. Spot check the addresses and names. (If you don't have specific names, don't solicit the prospect.) After you qualify your leads, you can use a number of computer technologies to market your goods and services.

Telemarketing

Telemarketing has emerged as one of the most cost-effective means of making initial contacts with your prospects. Your computer can make telemarketing less of a tedious task. Once the province of large corporations, automated telemarketing systems are now also accessible to small-scale entrepreneurs. Big Mouth, for example, is a relatively inexpensive add-in that allows your computer to make a series of telephone calls that pitch a message in your own voice.

Consider the following before you send your message to the entire country:

1. *The less said, the better.* To make your telemarketing effective, use it as a means of alerting customers or prospects about pending sales and other opportunities—no one wants one's telephone tied up with a long-winded pitch.
2. *Avoid prime calling times.* This may violate common sense, but the best time for you to reach people is when they are least likely to want to talk to you. They're busy doing something of far more concern to them—running their own business and servicing their own customers.

Fax "Blast"

The fax machine, like the personal computer, has become a standard in every office, and it can be used as an extremely effective means of communicating your sales message. For a small customer base, you can manually fax your message. For a larger base, however, you'll need an automated approach. One such approach involves using a fax board and a software package that allows you to fax the same information to multiple parties. Fax software packages vary in their capabilities; for example, some allow you to pull names and phone numbers from a database in a common file structure, such as dBASE. BitFax/SR, for example, creates phone books with DBF files. Anther program, WinFax Pro, ties your fax phone books into other applications that store name and address information.

Another approach, which unencumbers your computer, is to use an outside service such as MCI that will fax for you or to use a software package such as On The Go Fax by Ibis Software ($75). All you have to do is send by modem a text file with the solicitation and a database file with the names and phone numbers. For a fee, the company will handle the entire fax job. This approach works well when you have a significant number of faxes to be sent, and you don't want to tie up your computer or to stay at a fixed phone line location. (We'll talk about cellular modems in Chapter 11.) If your volume is high enough, and you can offer regular work, you may be able to negotiate an excellent rate.

Whether you do a manual fax campaign or a 15,000-piece automated fax "blast," observe the following for best results:

1. *Only use mass faxing for time-sensitive offers.* Anything perceived as fax "junk mail" will raise the ire of the recipient and probably squash a sale—even if the other party has interest in your product or service. After all, unlike junk mail, which can be thrown out unread, or telemarketing calls, which can be ended by hanging up the phone, recipients must incur part of the fax solicitation cost. Even though the actual outlay is trivial, the idea of paying for unwanted solicitations outrages many people. Therefore, never use the fax for primary solicitations. Instead, restrict it to "final close outs," "last chance for renewals," "last chance to register," etc.

2. *Keep it short.* Because you are costing your prospects and customers money, remember the purpose of the fax blast—to inform people of a fleeting opportunity. Also keep in mind the credibility issue—with the fax as commonplace as it is, a short solicitation conveys a sense of urgency better than a multiple page document does. One way to keep your fax blasts short is to skip the cover page and build the transmittal information into the solicitation. You will not only reduce your sending charges, but the recipient will observe that you have tried to minimize his or her cost.

Fax-Back

The previous techniques describe ways of reaching out. Here's a technique for "reaching in." Fax-back involves a PC equipped with special hardware, including a scanner, and software. You create or scan in documents, store them on the PC's hard disk, and assign them a box number. When a customer or prospect calls in to the inbound phone number, he or she is greeted by a human voice that explains the options and procedures for requesting documents. The caller is presented with a menu that lists various documents that are available for instant transmission. The caller uses the telephone keypad to select an item or group of items and to provide his or her fax machine's telephone number. The fax-back system will then transmit the requested documents. MarketFax offers a complete fax-back system for $10,000 and provides everything you need to run a fax-back system: 386 computer, voice board, scanner, modem, fax board, printer, tape backup, pre-installed software, and a table to put it all on. You need only boot up the system, scan in your documents, assign them box numbers and sit back while your fax-back system does all the hard work of waiting for your customers to call.

Although this is a book on portable selling, the computer hardware for a fax-back system is strictly home office bound. However, its capabilities do have a definite impact on the traveling sales representative. Imagine, while waiting at Chicago's O'Hare airport between flights, you call your office for messages. Among the usual messages is one of particular interest. Bill Smith has called with an inquiry about your new product. You want to follow up immediately, so you call Bill from the airport lounge. Halfway through your pitch, Bill says he really needs to see some technical specifications to properly evaluate your product. What can you do? Your client is ready to buy, and you are on your way to Omaha. Are you going to hang up on Bill and call your office to have them mail Bill the data? What if you're a one-man operation, or your partners are on the road as well? Are you going to wait until you get back from Omaha to follow up? Bill may decide on another product in the interim. With a fax-back system, you have another option. Simply ask Bill for his fax number and ask him to hold momentarily. You pick up the phone in the adjacent booth, call your fax-back number and key in the numbers assigned to the required documents and the number of Bill's fax machine. The documents are immediately on their way to Bill; thus you can complete your sales call with the necessary documents in your client's hand.

If you are a one-man operation, what happens to your client inquiries when you are on the road, on vacation, or out sick—when no one is minding the store? With a fax-back system as a backstop to your regular answering system, you can respond to your client's inquiries even when you are not in the office. The client is greeted with a polite and professional voice offering him the full range of your sales material immediately—no waiting for express delivery or the mail. The system maintains a detailed record of what material was sent to whom, thus you can easily follow up with additional material when you return.

Let's look at another scenario. Suppose that you place an ad for a new product in a trade magazine. Suddenly, you receive a tremendous response. Your incoming inquiries double, triple, and double again. You are overwhelmed; you receive one phone call after another. You begin to feel like the order-taker for the local pizza parlor during halftime at the Super Bowl. You need someone or something to handle the overflow: fax-back to the rescue. It can answer the surplus calls politely and professionally, but, unlike a simple answering machine, it can respond to your prospective client's current needs—more information. By properly wording your outgoing message, you can use the system to pre-qualify all incoming calls for a particular campaign.

The fax-back system is also a perfect complement for a catalog-based business with complicated products that require many pages of specifications or illustrations. Your catalog can be concise—containing just the essential product information, your marketing pitch, and a reference to the fax-back system box numbers pertaining to more complete product descriptions, pricing, illustrations, and so on. Your catalog is cheaper to print and mail in quantity and is not cluttered by a mass of detail. Your fax-back system provides the most up-to-date specifications and pricing to those clients who are truly interested—self-qualified leads.

An interesting use of a fax-back system is its capability to act like a private messaging system for your company. Because it has the capability to accept incoming faxes and to generate outgoing faxes, you can assign each sales rep a separate box number. You can transmit information from any fax machine (such as your portable PC's fax/modem) to the fax-back system at the home office and designate it for box 123, assigned to your colleague John. When John calls in, he can request all faxes waiting for box 123, and he will get your message forwarded to the fax/modem on his portable PC. Thus, your company has a complete fax-based messaging system.

A fax-back system will serve you best if you follow these suggestions:

1. *Keep the documents short.* Send people the information they need to make a purchasing decision. If you must send 10 pages, then send 10 pages. But remember, every page that you eliminate saves you time (shorter transmission) and increases your call volume (phone lines tied up less). Also, customers and prospects will appreciate paying for and dealing with less paper. When it comes to fax-back, short is best.

2. *Organize your fax-back presentation.* You don't want customers and prospects striving to organize the papers they have just received. Make sure that each transmittal tells a complete story. Begin with an introductory page/cover sheet that explains what they have received (a fax-back), and how they can receive additional information. Mention your company and its other products, too.

Direct Mail

A database of qualified leads is a mailing waiting to happen. If you have enough leads, consider using a program such as Professional Mail by Arc Tangent ($795) that provides comprehensive mail sorting and bundling information for the lowest bulk-rate mailing costs. Arc Tangent also offers two auxiliary packages: Zip++ ($195) and National Database ($195 /quarter). The former corrects ZIP codes and adds carrier route coding, and the latter itemizes addresses for the entire United States—9 million entries! When used in conjunction with Professional Mail, you can create virtually any mailing list based on basic ZIP code, SIC code, or other criteria. Regardless of the program used to store the information, consider the following general principles of direct mail.

1. *Always personalize your mail.* With today's mailmerge capabilities, there's no reason to ever send someone a "Dear Customer" or "President" letter; such greetings immediately label your correspondence as junk mail. While the mailmerge function might be intimidating, read your word processing software manual, and you may be pleasantly surprised as to its ease.

2. *Don't restrict your direct mail campaigns to selling products and services.* Traditionally, direct mail is used only to get an instant return (and hopefully one greater than the cost of the mailing). Although that is certainly a valid use for the selling technique, it is just one way to turn prospects into customers and customers into long-term supporters of your business. Use your mailing list to send company newsletters, copies of articles that you've clipped from newspapers, write-ups of customer solutions to common problems, and so on. In other words, use direct mail to stay in touch, to demonstrate your expertise, and to show your customers and prospects that you care—that you are more than just a "product pusher." Perhaps they won't place an immediate order when they receive the mailing, but the next time they are ready to buy, they will think of you as the vendor of choice.
3. *Make it easy to respond.* Whether you're sending a solicitation or an "FYI" ("for your information"), make it easy for the customer or prospect to respond. Include a postage paid card, list an 800 number, or list a fax-back number. Make it easy for someone to respond; you will be more likely to make a sale or gain a prospect who may buy from you at a later date.

Inside Advice

Respect your customers' and prospects' time. This is a cardinal rule that applies to all forms of prospect and customer outreach. Everyone is besieged with far more information than they can process; one study revealed that a single issue of *The New York Times* contains more information than a 16th century person had to process in an entire lifetime! When confronted with too much information, a person's impulse is to find the quickest way to get rid of it or ignore it. For the salesperson, this has serious implications. Most people are far more eager to part with your information than to listen to what you have to say. Be brief and persuasive and make yours a small contribution to their information burden. Meet the challenge, and you'll maximize your chances of getting through and making a sale.

■ ■ ■

4

Sales Automation Software

The field of software suitable for use by sales people has expanded, then recently contracted, as winner products have emerged. The annual directory of Sales Automation Software made available by the Sales Automation Association has decreased in size as the number of remaining vendors has diminished significantly. This directory can be obtained by calling (313) 278-5655.

The software that is appropriate for you depends on the tasks you want to accomplish. In the following list, you will see the expansion of software tasks that constitute sales automation. As your needs become clarified, you proceed down the list. Usually, beginners make the mistake of selecting software that doesn't allow room for growth. To be sure that you have a system enabling future growth, match your requirements with these functions.

Selecting the right software for your operation has become a task of selecting the right features from a wealth of options. To make matters more complicated, features with exactly the same name can be slanted in different directions. But, in this chapter, we will clarify these functions to make it easier for you to make a selection.

List Management	Lists used for mailing; usually mailing labels or simple lists
Contact Management	Lists used for tracking one-on-one contacts; usually for clubs or small business functions
Account Management	Databases used for tracking one-to-many relationships; usually for robust account management tasks
Sales Management	Databases with all of the preceding features plus sales reporting; usually for sales analysis and forecasts
Sales & Marketing Management	Databases using sales data in marketing; usually for competitive analysis or new product design information

Since no two businesses are exactly alike, no single solution is appropriate for all salespeople on the road. The key is to look at the features offered by a number of software packages and evaluate the relative importance of each as it pertains to your business. For example, if outgoing telemarketing is a key part of your business, a critical feature of your contact management software is its capability to automatically generate outbound calls. Many of the packages we will review offer some version of this feature but at many levels of implementation. At one extreme is software that will rapidly process a list of telephone numbers until it gets a connection—only then will it place the prospect's information on the screen for the salesman to make his or her pitch. At the other extreme is software that automatically dials the phone number from the current record only. Both generate outbound calls—one totally automatically and the other virtually manually. Which is appropriate for your business? Only you can tell.

In deciding what type of software to use you need to look for sales management features as follows:

Sales Cycle Tracking Tracking the status of each customer through the sales cycle from lead to close of sale; determining whether your clients or customers are currently active or inactive. Breaking down the cycle into more levels is valuable in long sales cycles. Tracking what percent of your prospects are in which phase can be a powerful management technique.

Account Tracking Tracking multiple decision makers in your account; knowing how large or small the target company is, in how many offices you might make a sale, etc.; tracking SIC codes, demographics, and all related account contacts. Who reports to whom, how many decision makers are there, and what are their concerns are key elements of account information.

Sales Management Providing on-line information such as scripts, product descriptions, and order entry capability for sales people; determining where your sales are coming from today and where you want them to come from in the future. Tracking milestones achieved in the process, sales event tracking, and further breaking down the steps in the sales cycle to better define their status is also important. For example, you may need to know how many of your prospects have gotten a proposal or demonstration from you.

Sales & Marketing Management Using the information collected by field sales people to make marketing decisions; determining win/loss ratios, who your competitors are, where your best leads come from, what advertising works best, and why. Launching sales initiatives from this marketing information is a key outcome of the process.

Evaluating Software

Are you prepared to change? A properly implemented contact management tool is much more than just a database for storing names, telephone numbers and perhaps a date or two. It will profoundly change the way you do business on a day-to-day basis. You must choose to exchange your current laissez faire methods of operation for the disciplined approach dictated by the software you select. In this fashion, each package has its own attitude towards the user.

Some are extremely rigid, forcing you to address overdue work, follow tasks in the assigned order, and complete one task before starting the next. Others have a more forgiving nature, allowing you to easily postpone and reschedule work. Your choice will depend on what you want or need. Be sure to evaluate the tone of the software in the same way you would evaluate a roommate—it can be your closest friend or worst enemy.

What is your primary objective? Before you begin to evaluate sales automation software, you need to know what you want it to do. All of the packages provide a myriad of features, but some are better at one feature than the rest. Don't buy a condensed telemarketing package if you really want a follow-up scheduler.

How computer knowledgeable do you want to become? Assuming that you are not in PC hardware or software sales, you probably don't want to become an expert in sales automation software. In general, there is a trade off between ease of use and system flexibility. If you have no interest in developing a custom database specification, you should choose a package with a default or fixed file structure that meets your needs. Likewise, you should determine that the system has a logical, consistent user interface that permits you to use its functions with a minimum of effort. A program that has been slapped together will be evident in its inconsistent structure.

If you are like most users and refuse to read the user manual, will you be able to learn the system via an on-line tutorial or from formal training classes? What sort of support is provided as part of the purchase price—full-time technical support personnel or sales reps more intent on the next sale than supporting the last?

Comfort and Speed of User Interface

If you are going to spend extended periods of time working with your selected software, you need to be very concerned about the legibility of the screen, especially if you are working on a portable computer with an LCD screen. Several of the packages have special screen drivers that optimize the LCD display; others will only produce washed-out shades of gray. If your basic use is looking up client records in your master database, you will need to be concerned with the speed of access. The packages vary considerably in this standard procedure. Be sure to test your selected software with a database of the same size as you intend to maintain. You can't evaluate a package's performance with only five test records if you plan on using it with thousands. If you don't have test data that you can import into a demo, ask the vendor to supply the test data.

Flexibility and Customizability

No two businesses have the same needs. Some need to track multiple contact names within a single company. Some need much personal information about their clients. Others need to maintain detailed financial information for each client. One product can meet all these differing requirements by allowing you to customize one or more fields to your specific requirements. You could define one field to be your client's secretary's name and another field to be the last product ordered. The degree of flexibility offered is represented by the number of customizable fields, whether they are of fixed format (text, numbers, and dates) or variable format, and whether they are of fixed or variable length. In general, more is better up to the point of user confusion—beyond 15 or 20 is just marketing competition.

Cost Considerations

If you look at the amount of your time that will be invested in your new system, the value of your data, the information you will be able to extract from it, and the income produced by new sales resulting from your system, the cost of the software itself pales in comparison. Most systems cost between $100–500 for a single-user version with a few high-end systems approaching $1,000. Although this is not loose change, it is not a significant consideration when compared to other factors.

Security Considerations

Information is power, and, if it falls into the wrong hands, it can be dangerous. When you are carrying your data with you on the road, you are exposing yourself to accidental loss or theft. If you are flying to Las Vegas for a convention of widget manufacturers, you can bet that one or more of your competitors are on the same flight—maybe in the next seat. You can't afford to give them the opportunity to swipe your hard-earned client files while you visit the restroom prior to landing. Your files must be encrypted and password protected before you take them on the road, and you must be careful not to expose your data to prying eyes.

Ease of Importing and Exporting Data

We discussed the many sources for sales leads in Chapters 1 and 2. They are of little use if you cannot incorporate them into your sales automation system. Virtually all contact management packages offer one or more methods for importing data from outside sources. The most prevalent method uses the lowest common denominator strategy of comma delimited ASCII files. This technique works fine if your source data is in the same file layout as the target file. If not, you will need a more sophisticated import facility, a file conversion utility or a vendor-assisted data conversion. Make sure that you have covered this base before you buy. If you have an existing database system, find out if the vendor will convert and load your data as part of the sales agreement or for a small additional fee.

Reports

Although the sales rep on the road typically views his contact management software as strictly an on-line facility, there will always be a place for hard copy reports—if only to print a hard copy of today's appointments. Many of the contact management packages offer both an impressive suite of predefined reports and a facility for creating your own formats. Perhaps more important than format flexibility is the ability to define which records are included in a particular report or mailing process. In many ways, the flexibility of record selection is tied to the flexibility of the user definable fields. If you can define a field for a client's birthday, you should be able to select all records with a birthday in May so that you can send out birthday cards.

What to say when you are on the spot. Not only should your selected software allow you to quickly find a client's record as soon as you answer the phone, but it should assist you in addressing his or her questions and concerns. Many of the packages offer a scripting option that allows you to predefine answers to specific questions or outgoing sales pitches, available at the touch of a key. Some systems offer sophisticated branching scripts that allow you to zero in on a specific problem or opportunity by selecting various options as you conduct the telephone conversation.

Word Processing

Although none of the word processors included with contact management software will threaten the market share of the specialized full-featured word processors such as WordPerfect or Word for Windows, they do offer the convenience of being directly integrated with your primary application. If you are spending your day with your sales automation package, it is very convenient to jot a quick note or to create a mailmerge document without ever leaving your primary application. If you are already wedded to a particular word processor, you should be sure that your selected package can export its data directly into the proper format for a secondary merge file. This will allow you to avoid the complications of converting data each time you want to do a client mailing. In addition, you should check to see whether you can load your selected word processor "on top" of the contact management package. Most packages do a fairly good job of getting out of the way when you want to load a word processor or spreadsheet program; some do not.

Regarding Windows Applications

There has been a lot of talk recently focusing on the new Windows product from Microsoft. Your sales automation software need not be Windows based, because the features of the new Windows are not usually needed. Recognize that Windows runs with MS-DOS and is an add-on product. Windows offers two primary functions they didn't have before: multitasking (the capability to run two programs simultaneously) and a screen design or interface that uses pictures and icons rather than the typewritten commands. Neither of these functions is typically needed by the field salesperson.

It is important to remember to pick the right application software to fit your tasks before you consider the operating system software. By that, we mean pick the sales automation software for your task and then select the right support equipment and software to run it.

Write down the tasks you need accomplished first. Then select the application software that accomplishes these tasks!

Automated Processing

The purpose of committing your time, data, and soul to your new computerized contact management system is to have the computer do some of your work for you. A whole raft of opportunities are available—schedule tracking, beeping alarms for follow-up tasks, automatic roll over of uncompleted tasks and so on. Each package provides a laundry list of automated features—make sure that your choice has the key features for your business and that you can ignore or turn off the features that you do not want to use.

Portability—will it fit and will it link? When considering the portability of the application, three issues come immediately to mind: screen legibility, storage requirements and shareability. We have already discussed the legibility issue. For more information about screen hardware options, see Chapter 6. The second potential stumbling block is storage requirements. If your portable has no hard disk, can you fit the program onto floppies or load it onto a RAM disk (RAM emulating a hard disk). If not, you are out of luck unless you upgrade your memory or add an external hard disk. (And a hard disk adds one more thing to lug through the airports and explain to security: "No, ma'am, it doesn't take pictures; I cannot open it; and I certainly do not want to pass it though the metal detector. Yes, ma'am, I guess I would prefer the bus.")

More subtle but perhaps most significant is the program's capability to work with other users in your company. If you are one of many sales reps in the field, does it make sense for all of you to share information? If so, how can you pass data back and forth? Some packages offer sophisticated merge-purge routines that allow users in the field to send data via modem to the home office and then receive by modem an updated master list. Some even allow the home office-based sales manager to reassign records to specific sales reps.

If you are responsible for considering the selection of software for an entire sales organization, it is important to consider connecting them together in some way. Connecting the sales reps with each other or with the home office is key to improving their productivity. Consider the Ally Data Link product, for example. The optional Sales Ally module is a two-way information highway that lets sales managers and sales representatives send and receive sales-related information over a modem from the field to the home office.

Ally Data Link works with Sales Ally to allow field sales representatives to "off-load" their sales activity information, thus eliminating the need for manual reporting. It's a real timesaver. Further, this system allows the home office to distribute new sales leads to the field over the modem, ready for calling!

To Network or Not

If you spend time in a central office, the question of networking comes into play. If you require simultaneous access to a common database, it is the only way to go. Only through network control procedures is the integrity of the database protected and the most current data available to all users. When looking at software packages, look for a smooth transition path to the network version of the software if that option seems forthcoming.

Special Features

Many of the packages offer special features, often as an add-in option. For example, several offer client invoicing and a simple accounts receivable option. Others offer expense tracking and reporting modules. If you are planning to use the included word processor, you will probably want to include a spelling checker, and so on. Look at the list realistically. What do you need, and what do you desire? How important is each feature to the central objective of the system? If you plan to use a system only for outgoing sales calls, then don't pick it for its spelling checker.

Linked to these add-in modules are sophisticated reporting tools. For example, if you are tracking sales within an invoicing system, you can also generate sales performance reports. Additionally, if you are reporting pending sales and their probability of closing, you can generate a sales forecast report.

Repetitive task automation. Anyone who has spent a significant amount of time knocking on doors knows that the process involves a number of repetitive tasks. The same applies to sales automation software. Periodic updating of records is a requirement of all software systems, and the process can become very tedious indeed. Likewise, you may perform the same sequences of keystrokes repetitively throughout the day. To reduce the repetitiveness, many contact management packages include a macro processing facility. In simple terms, the system records your keystrokes into a special disk file and assigns a unique key combination that can be used to execute the key sequence exactly as it was recorded.

In a similar vein, you may frequently want to create similar reports and queries—e.g. pulling all active accounts that haven't purchased in the last three months for an inquiry letter. Wouldn't it be nice if the system remembered how to create the desired extract and allowed you to recall it with a few keystrokes? Fortunately, most of the systems provide such a facility.

No two clients or prospects are exactly alike. Each client is unique, and you may want to keep unique information about him or her as part of the standard record. In these situations, the capability to attach one or more variable length notes to a record is critical. For some records, you may have little information or little activity, while for others you may have pages and pages of notes. Your selected systems should be able to easily handle such disparate storage demands easily and efficiently.

Do phone numbers really change when you are on the road? They do if you move into different area codes. Calls that were local when initiated from your home base now become long distance when you are out of town. Your software should be able to recognize your local area code (you must specify it) and then include or exclude the area codes entered into your database as required when making calls. Likewise, you should be able to specify a special dialing prefix to escape the binds of a hotel's pbx or to access a special long distance service.

The $2,000 calculator. Using a calculator to figure numbers you need to enter into your computer looks as ridiculous as calculating the same figures by hand on the back of an envelope. Your software should be able to pop up a full-featured calculator and calendar at the push of a button, allowing you to calculate a key figure or look up the desired data and paste the results directly into your input screen.

Looks Do Matter

Nothing identifies incoming mail as "junk" more than a poorly printed dot matrix label. You may as well address it to "Occupant" for all the attention it will receive. In today's competitive environment, you must use every tool to get your message in front of your client. Often, this means directly printing an address onto an envelope using a high-quality printer such as a laser printer. Your selected software should support a variety of printers.

Making the Decision

The preceding guidelines provide a framework for making a wise software purchase decision. We will not hide our prejudice for Sales Ally by Scherrer Resources, Inc. The clear presence of the founder of the company as one of the authors of this book quickly belies our impartiality. Sales Ally has won several industry awards, as have others including ACT! by Contact Software. We also make mention of products such as The Maximiser contact manager by Richmond Technologies and Software, TeleMagic telemarketing software by Remote Control International, and Instant Office office management software by Dilworth Software.

Only you can determine which of these capable packages is the best fit for your needs. Follow the guidelines listed in this chapter, insist on talking to current clients and, above all, insist on trying the software before you commit your business future to it.

■ ■ ■

5

Time Management and Scheduling

Timing is everything, especially in sales. You need not only be on time for scheduled appointments, but you must constantly make follow-up calls and carry out activities that demonstrate to the customer or prospect that you're not just a product pusher—you are someone who is there as a partner and a problem solver.

A number of computer software products can help you improve your sales effectiveness by helping you manage your schedule. These generally fall into the software genre known as "PIMs" (personal information managers). PIMs enhance your personal productivity by enabling you to track your time, manage appointments, create to-do lists, and maintain address books. Sales automation software such as Sales Ally, Smart Office by EZ Data, and ask Sam by askSam Systems all contain scheduling and time-management functions as part of their integrated sales support systems.

Personal information managers range from simple electronic appointment books, such as the one built into Windows or WordPerfect Office, to highly sophisticated programs, such as Agenda. The high-end PIMs enable you to input vast quantities of schedule and customer data and generate comprehensive task lists. In between, you'll find a variety of programs that generate "rolling" to-do lists and other useful reports. (On Time is a good example of such a program). Let's take a closer look at these three types of PIMs and your uses for them.

Simple Schedulers

We all keep paper trails of our appointments, whether we use an appointment book or scraps of napkins and envelopes. An electronic scheduler performs the same functions as the appointment book. The input screen generally resembles a traditional appointment book, with time increments starting in the morning and ending in the evening. (Many allow you to indicate whether you want to enter information by day, week, or month.) Next to each time or date, you type in what you need to do, whom you need to call, or whom you need to see. Your computer will chime, beep, or provide a visual message when it's time to perform the task.

This approach to managing your schedule is fine if you spend a lot of time in front of your computer, or if you are on the road and have the time (and discipline) to boot up your laptop fairly frequently. If you are not in a position to constantly access your computer, however, you'll find that the purely electronic scheduler is actually more of a nuisance.

Other types of schedulers allow you to print reports that mimic traditional appointment books, and some software programs even provide stock forms for popular products offered by Day Timers, Day Runner, and other suppliers. By using your software program to print your schedule, you can constantly make changes without crossing out or erasing previous entries. Again, however, you must make a commitment to the computer; if you maintain half of your schedule electronically and half on paper, you'll wind up with...half a schedule!

Finally, consider one other type of "quasi-PIM"—the calendar generator. This category of software, typified by Calendar Creator Plus, generates daily, weekly, or monthly calendars. The advantage is that you can quickly get a visual sense of how you will be spending your time. Note that many project management schedulers also print calendars in addition to GANTT and PERT charts—but only after you have input project details through a potentially laborious process.

To-Do List Generators

If you want to go beyond simple schedulers, consider a program that manages to-do lists. As you "check off" items that you have completed, the program updates the list; incomplete items roll over to the next work day. Many of the PIMs in this category allow you to assign a priority to the various items on your list and organize them accordingly. Finally, some PIMs, such as Pack Rat and Current, integrate to-do lists with schedulers, phone books, and other components.

As with the simple schedulers, you need a certain amount of discipline to make to-do list generators assist you in your sales efforts. If you do not constantly update them, you will not get an accurate picture of what needs to be done. On the other hand, if you are juggling numerous sales-related tasks and appointments, a well-managed to-do list can be a blueprint for effective short-and long-term action.

High-End PIMs

Imagine a program that allows you to enter tasks "on the fly" and then group the tasks by common names, places, or dates. For instance, let's say that you have the following tasks: "touch base with J.G.B. Company on April 10 and inquire about inventory level," "mail copy of our newsletter to J.G.B. Company with personal note on May 3," and "prepare new competitive bids for J.G.B. Company by May 14." Now imagine instantly pulling out a list of all tasks related to J.G.B. Company—or any other person, place, time, specific meeting, etc. This is precisely the kind of feat that Lotus Development Corporation's Agenda performs. Agenda allows you to enter tasks and categorize them any way you want. You can view your data in to-do list form or according to projects, people, meetings, sales campaigns, etc.

Another program, Grandview, also allows you to assign categories to tasks. Grandview is unique in that it displays all tasks in the form of a structured outline. For each headline or item in the outline, you assign categories such as "high-, medium-, or low-priority," "date due," "customer name," etc. You can then display all of the high-priority tasks, all of the tasks related to a particular customer, all of the tasks to be performed in May, and so on.

The ability to assign categories to entries and then create different views is immensely powerful, especially if you are carrying out many activities for your customers and prospects. You can randomly jot notes or appointment dates pertaining to a particular project, a pending order, a presentation, etc. The software will organize the data for you, making it easy to put it into an action plan. Your action plan can be structured on a daily, weekly or monthly basis. The beauty of this approach is that you capture important ideas without worrying if they fit into the "big picture"—simply switch to the view of the customer or prospect in question and then make decisions about when and how to implement a specific plan.

High-end PIMs can have a lengthy learning curve—especially Agenda. Even an experienced user will require a certain amount of "playing time" until he or she can productively use the software. Also, the system's powerful flexibility is its own trap—you will need time and skill to plan out the kind of system you want to develop by asking yourself what kind of information you ought to be capturing for the categories, how the categories relate to each other and, ultimately, how you will use the information in your short- and long-term planning.

Using PIMs To Enhance Your Sales Effectiveness

Whichever type of PIM you select, be sure to capture the following kinds of information:

- The basics—customer and prospect meetings, internal staff meetings, etc.
- Sales call follow-ups and other "ticklers."

- Opportunities to maintain on-going communications with customers and prospects—e.g. to remind them of upcoming events.
- Project milestones and completion dates. Although you'll probably want to use a dedicated project management program to track the development of a large-scale sales campaign or presentation, a PIM can be extremely useful for keeping tabs on the progress of sales reports, sales presentations, and other projects with multiple components.
- Estimates of customer reorder dates. By making a sales inquiry at the right time, you will demonstrate your knowledge of the customer's operation and a commitment to providing top-notch service.
- Geographical proximity of your sales appointments. With programs like Agenda or Grandview, you can create a category that specifies the distance from your base office. You could, for example, assign geographic zones or categories such as 5 to 10 miles, 10 to 20, etc. You could then create views of all the appointments within a 5 to 10 mile radius. A quick "sanity" check of your schedule will point out if your schedule is overloaded, requiring you to travel at Mach 3 to make all your meetings.
- Important dates for customers and prospects, such as start-of-sale dates, final sale dates, trade show dates, conference dates, and even government form-filing dates if appropriate. Although your customers may already know about conference and filing dates, they will appreciate the fact that you are on top of their business needs and will regard you as an important supplier of information.

Inside Advice

- *Don't assume that a PIM will solve time management problems.* If you cannot manage your time manually, a PIM will only mask the problems and provide the *illusion* of order. The underlying chaos may eventually lead to lost sales opportunities.

- *Establish goals for your PIM.* What do you want to accomplish? Are you just trying to stay on top of follow-up calls, or do you need to track complex projects and schedules? Select a software program with the appropriate capabilities. As with any software product, buying on the bottom tier because you will "never need any more capabilities" is usually cheaper but costlier. Once you realize the power of PIMs, you may want more capabilities, thus spending additional sums for a new program and undergoing another learning curve.
- *Build your PIM incrementally.* Start with your basic schedule, and then add more complex levels of information. If you try to reorganize your life overnight, something may slip through the cracks, and you may get discouraged.
- *Enter complete data.* The more detailed the information you enter into a PIM, the more useful the output. For example, when you enter follow-up calls into a scheduler, be sure to enter the direct and alternate phone numbers of the people with whom you will be speaking, as well as the names of their assistants. Also, jot down any "tidbits" you intend to pass on in addition to the main objective of the call. This may seem trivial, but it could ensure that your call achieves its results.

In short, treat PIMs like any software category. They can do an admirable job of automating your sales tasks but only to the extent that you are using them effectively. Look at PIMs as opportunities for freeing up time. You can use this time to hone your sales skills and plans, make more contacts that can lead to lucrative sales, and provide better service to your customers—these, of course, are ultimately the keys to more effective selling.

■ ■ ■

6

Sales Presentations

As a busy sales representative, you have the difficult challenge of presenting your products or services to an equally busy client. Time is at a premium, and you must compete with the many distractions of a busy work day. You have to seize the buyer's attention and keep it with a sales message that is professional, quick, and to the point.

An easy and successful sales technique is to create a slide presentation and to use your portable computer as a slide projector. If you are presenting to a single buyer or a small group, your laptop computer screen may be sufficient. In fact, by grouping all the viewers around a single screen, you can often add to the intimacy and drama of a sales presentation. For larger groups, you will have to use a projection system to enable all players to see your message clearly.

Creating a slide show on a PC is cheap and extremely easy. Some of the best software—Aldus Persuasion and Lotus' Freelance Graphics for Windows—literally take longer to install than to create the first presentation. The quality of your presentation depends on the hardware and software you choose, and, as with many things in life, better costs more. However, if you already own a portable PC with a reasonably clear backlit LCD VGA screen and Windows 3.1, you can create a truly impressive show just by adding Persuasion or Freelance. More importantly, their ease of use will allow you to focus on your message and not on the technology.

Some very respectable presentation packages work under DOS, most notably Dan Bricklin's Demo from Software Garden and Lotus' Freelance Graphics. However, the future in this arena is definitely Windows-based.

Other options exist for creating slide shows. Although somewhat more difficult and time consuming, you can use your word processor or spreadsheet program to create presentations. We will look at the process of creating a sales presentation using one of the specialty products (Lotus' Freelance for Windows), a word processor, and a spreadsheet program.

Creating a Presentation with Freelance Graphics for Windows

Lotus' Freelance for Windows is one of several new programs specifically designed to make presentation preparation and delivery as easy as possible. You can quickly enter text, create charts and graphs, and add images to create a sequence of slides for your presentation. You can print the final screens with a black-and-white or color laser printer directly on acetate for an overhead projector; you can prepare files for a service bureau's or your own slide printer; or you can create a slide show on your portable PC.

The first step in creating a sales presentation with Freelance is selecting a general appearance for each of the individual slides. Lotus provides more than 60 professionally developed SmartMaster templates consisting of nine different but coordinated page layouts. For example, Figure 6.1 shows a graph page of the Deco SmartMaster design, and Figure 6.2 shows the corresponding completed slide. The nine coordinated templates of each design provide ample flexibility for most presentations, and the consistent overall design of the SmartMaster set provides cohesion to the total presentation.

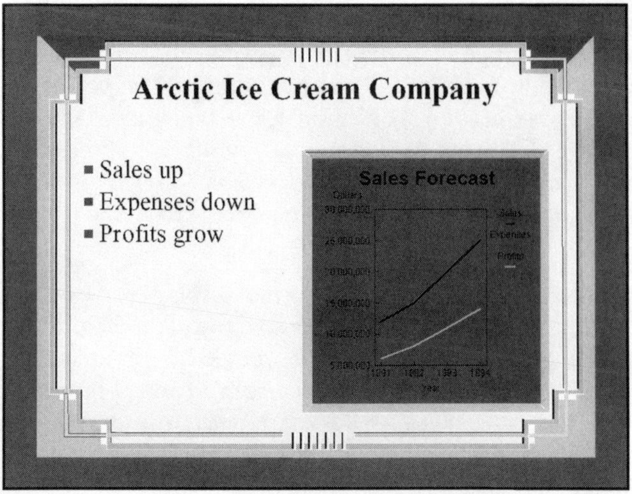

Figure 6.1 Freelance SmartMaster page with place holders

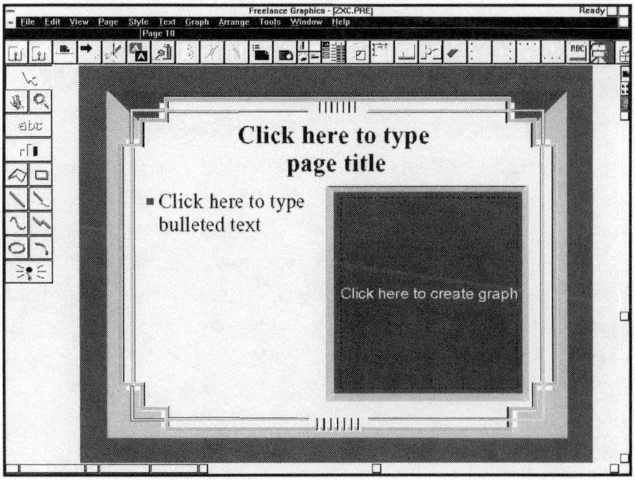

Figure 6.2 Freelance SmartMaster page with user's text inserted

Display Options

As described earlier, you can print your slides, or you can display the images directly on your PC. The latter option allows you to create an animated presentation. You control how one image fades into the next based on either a timed interval or your cue. This can prove to be a superior presentation tool for small groups in which all members of the audience can see the same screen and truly participate in the presentation.

A larger audience requires a large format display. You can use either a passive LCD panel with an existing overhead projector (it uses the light and optics of the overhead projector) or an active LCD projector (it contains its own light source and optics) to enlarge your presentation. Although each has its strengths, the ultimate decision will probably be based on cost—the active projectors cost several times that of the passive panels and deliver larger (up to 100 inches diagonally) and clearer displays. In either case, you are cautioned to check out the projector with your particular portable computer and display adapter to ensure compatibility before hitting the road.

Creating a Presentation with a Word Processor or a Spreadsheet

Specialty products such as Lotus' Freelance and Aldus Persuasion have greatly simplified the process of creating presentations, but they have their costs. Not only do they cost several hundreds of dollars, but they take up a lot of space—Freelance for Windows requires 11 megabytes of space for a full installation. Therefore, you should not overlook the capability of software that you already own for creating presentations. A word processor with proportional font capabilities can be used to create a hard copy presentation, and that hard copy can be converted to an overhead projection acetate at most copy shops. If you are using a true "WYSIWYG" word processor (the screen displays exactly what it is going to print), you can even create a rudimentary slide show by placing each "slide" on a separate page and using the PgDn/PgUp keys to move between them.

Spreadsheets can be used to create fairly sophisticated presentations. Lotus 1-2-3, Borland's Quattro Pro and Microsoft's Excel all support a rudimentary slide show facility. For example, with Lotus 1-2-3, you can turn off the framework and control panel displays and create individual "page" displays of bulleted text. Additionally, you can create a wide variety of graphs. You can even import clip art and place and size it anywhere on the worksheet. To display your presentation, use the PgDn/PgUp keys to move through your presentation one page or "slide" at a time. Using a worksheet allows you to customize your presentations for a particular customer via the dynamic link feature. For example, if you keep your customer's name, sales volume, and product preferences in a Lotus worksheet, you can link the cells in the text portion of the display to the name and product cells and use the sales data to create the graph. Remember, nothing sells like personal attention.

The key to creating presentations is to quickly master the technology of choice so that it becomes a familiar tool. This allows you to concentrate on your message and not on the technical process required to make your presentations look great. Any of these tools can greatly facilitate this process, helping you to present your products in the best light and to close the sale.

Using Sales Presentation Tools To Enhance Your Sales Effectiveness

Be sure to remember the following regardless of the presentation tool you select:

Keep the text to a minimum—just state the key points.

A picture is only worth a thousand words when it is clear enough to be grasped instantly. If you need to explain it, it is not clear enough.

You only have one chance to capture your audience's attention. If you lose it, it is difficult to regain.

If your message is full of details, provide your audience with hard copies of your slides.

Keep the number of bulleted items on a single slide to a minimum—usually no more than six.

Make sure that all of the bullets on a single slide are related and are of the same level of significance in your presentation. If not, consider regrouping them by level of importance and/or creating subsidiary slides.

Visibility of Portable Computer Screens

Portable computers are available with a wide variety of display screens ranging from simple reflective LCD to active matrix color and gas plasma. The basic advantages and disadvantages of each are as follows:

	Advantages	Disadvantages
MONOCHROME		
Reflective LCD	Cheapest	Very poor viewing angle
	Good battery operation	No low-light visibility
Backlit Supertwist LCD	Low cost	Reasonable, but not great, viewing angle
	Reasonable battery operation	
Gas Plasma	Very good monochrome visibility	No battery operation
COLOR		
Passive Color LCD	Lower cost than active matrix	Poor viewing angle Washed out colors

	Advantages	Disadvantages
Active Matrix Color LCD	Very good color	Very high cost
	Reasonable viewing angle	Relatively poor battery performance

Most screens can be very difficult to read under certain lighting conditions. If you are using your portable for a presentation, make sure that your audience can see the screen clearly. Watch out for the following:

- Viewing angle
- Reflections
- Contrast
- Overall brightness

Monochrome

The most common screen technology for battery operated monochrome notebook and laptop computers is super-twist LCD (liquid crystal display—similar to the display used for most digital watches). This technology uses reflected ambient room light and gives excellent contrast under reasonable lighting (bright overhead source in a not overly bright room). It provides clear visibility when faced head on, and it delivers very poor visibility under dim lighting conditions.

Beware of "super deals" on notebooks and laptops—especially from volume discounters. Generally, the displays are inferior, older non-supertwist LCD displays that produce an abysmal display as compared with current technology.

Many newer LCD models are "backlit"—they contain their own light source behind the LCD display. Backlit screens are good for viewing under dim light but are difficult to see at wide angles. Other monochrome models use gas plasma technology that produces a crisp, amber screen, generates its own light, and provides visibility from a wide viewing angle. The gas plasma display is generally more expensive and is strictly limited to AC-power operation because of its high power consumption.

Color

Recent developments have added active and passive color matrix LCD screens to portable computers, providing full color VGA and super VGA displays to the sales representative on the road. As LCD technology, they suffer from limited viewing angles, and as new technology, they suffer from extremely high costs. Despite these limitations, the active matrix LCD color technology produces astounding displays

Which technology is best for you?

If you are limited to battery operation, you will be restricted to LCD technology—color or monochrome. (Plasma displays consume too much electricity for battery operation.)

If your message requires the added punch of color and if you can afford it, go ahead with a color screen purchase, but remember, as new technology, the cost will drop significantly, and the quality will improve in the next few years. Also remember that color that appears washed out could convey the wrong message for certain products. Newer models such as the NEC Ultralite SL/25C have overcome the washed-out appearance but again at higher costs.

Be sure to look at the specific model you are considering. View the screen under different lighting and from different angles. Pull together a group of four or five people and watch the screen from the edge of the group or over someone else's shoulder. Many dealers allow you to test a model for a day or two before purchasing it, and most mail order vendors grant liberal return policies if the model proves unsatisfactory. Before you order, be sure to analyze the return policy, especially to disclose any restocking or return fees.

Portable Projection Systems

When you are presenting to a group of more than four or five, you cannot rely on your portable's screen no matter how clear it may be. Larger groups require larger displays. Three different technologies can be employed for larger groups.

1. A first option is the ubiquitous CRT (cathode ray tube) display used with most desktop computer systems. Although we certainly do not recommend carting a CRT monitor with you on your sales calls, its use during your presentation may be a viable option. Many clients may have a VGA-compatible monitor available at their office and, with advance notice, would be willing to lend it to you for your presentation. Most portable PCs sold today include a standard VGA (high resolution color) port to which you can readily attach a client's color or monochrome VGA display. If your computer has a non-standard display system (e.g. the higher resolution, super VGA), be sure that you can switch it to a VGA emulation if required by your client's monitor.

2. For large sales presentations, a second option is an overhead projector with a transparent display filter. Using the projector's light source and optics coupled with the LCD imaging device, you can project crisp images in black and white or color onto a standard slide projection screen. One new model produced by Sharp (QA-1050) provides full-VGA resolution with more than 185,000 colors and supports full-motion color. It also includes an intelligent remote control system that enables you to control the pace of your presentation.

NOTE

The LCD projection panel requires a standard overhead projector to provide the light source and display optics. Beware that all overhead projectors are not created equal. Some generate considerable heat that can cause loss of contrast with the heat-sensitive LCD panel. Others use a reflecting light system that bounces the light from above off a reflecting surface under the LCD panel. This process generates a less crisp image than projectors with the light source located below the LCD panel. If you are purchasing a new projector, be certain to test it with your specific LCD panel to ensure image quality. If you are planning to use a client's display system, be aware that there may be some quality reduction.

A third option avoids compatibility problems between the LCD panel and the projection system by incorporating both within the same unit. Recent technological breakthroughs have produced a truly portable projection system. Panasonic produces a compact projector (Model PT-10L) weighing only 6.6 pounds and capable of projecting a full-color image up to 70 inches measured diagonally (see Figure 6.3), and a slightly larger model weighing 30 pounds and projecting an image up to 100 inches measured diagonally. Note that to use these products, you will also have to purchase a VGA-to-video converter.

Figure 6.3 Lightweight portable projector—Panasonic PT-10L

7

Quote Developement

The advent of the portable PC has introduced a powerful tool for closing a sale—the capability to generate immediately a custom quote and associated documentation in your client's office. This reduces client excuses: "I have to see it in writing," or "I'll get back to you." With a combination of word processors, spreadsheets, and forethought, you can be ready to respond to any twist or turn thrown in the way of closing a deal—all in real time without losing the attention of your client.

Let's look at the components of a hypothetical deal. Suppose that you are in the business of selling industrial cleaning equipment to the power generating industry. Your products range from standard cleansers to high-tolerance solvents used to clean turbine blades. Most of your sales are repetitive based on an annual price quote with an open purchase order. You try to meet with clients three months prior to their contract renewal date to negotiate the new rates and quantity pricing. Although your pricing has some leeway for deal making, it is basically volume-discount oriented. It gets complicated only because different products are eligible for different discounts, and the contract as a whole is eligible for a discount based on the total annual commitment. The terms of the contract are fairly standard, but because your clients are regulated industries in certain states, a lot of boilerplate language is required to assuage the appetites of the local legal community.

Before you purchased a portable computer, the sales cycle took several months with as many client visits as necessary to negotiate price and volume commitments and translate the resulting figures into hand-drafted proposals and contracts. Each iteration included several rounds of language reworking due to the inevitable errors that creep into any newly drafted document.

Now let's imagine a different scenario. You walk into your client's office for the annual renewal meeting with your portable PC and set it up in the conference room so that all parties can easily see the screen. You begin the first step in your automated quote system—a simple spreadsheet with an input column for volume commitments, a parallel column of discounted prices, the extended totals, the contract subtotal, the contract volume discount, and the final contract price.

The simplicity of the screen display belies the potentially complicated logic behind the numbers. As you discuss order quantities with your client, you enter the values into the volume commitment column of the spreadsheet. As you enter different commitment values, the discounted price changes automatically as per your standard price sheet. The extended prices are calculated along with the subtotal, contract discount, and total price. Your client can see instantly how the changes affect the bottom line. You and your client are able to pursue the mutual objective of getting him or her the best overall discount while guaranteeing you the highest order commitment.

After coming up with what you both believe to be the best possible deal, you ask the computer to perform a simple optimization calculation. Using the spreadsheet's built-in Solver program, you ask the program to seek the optimal mix of products and volumes that meet your client's minimum and maximum limits and produce the largest discount (coincidently producing the highest total dollar commitment for you). Your trusty portable chugs away for a few moments and then recommends that you modify the quantities slightly, saving your client another one-half percent. All of this has taken place before your client's ever-widening eyes. Never before has a vendor brought the black box calculator out into the light, let alone ask it to recommend a better deal for the client.

Your client is truly impressed and readily agrees to the basic commitment. Now, you must overcome the next hurdle of getting the terms into acceptable contract form. Knowing that you have crossed the difficult bridge already, you swiftly shift into your word processing software and retrieve the standard form contract. Your client is astounded to see that the contract on the screen already contains the price and sales figures to which he or she has just committed. You check your state-by-state special clause cross reference and find that your client's state requires the standard indemnification clause, so with two quick keystrokes, you insert the necessary text. After one final review, you instruct the system to print the document on your portable printer and out spews the final contract ready for both of your signatures. No typographical errors exist, as all the clauses have been reviewed previously by both your legal department and the state's. You have nothing left to do but sign and move on to the next prospect.

Several key technologies are introduced in this scenario, but nothing is beyond the range of widely available software. Let's look at the specifics. The spreadsheet quotation calculator is a simple input form with a lookup table containing the pricing breakpoints for each product. As you enter the volume figures, the worksheet looks up the associated price and places it in the unit cost column before calculating the extended cost. The same technique is used for the total contract discount. By entering the buyer's limits for each product line, you use the spreadsheet's built-in Solver program to perform an optimization under constraints. In other words, you find the best answer by logical trial and error.

You can switch to your word processor in several ways, one of which is to use the Windows operating environment. This environment supports two key concepts. Multiprocessing allows you to load your word processor and spreadsheet at the same time and toggle between them with a hot-key combination. Dynamic Data Exchange (DDE) allows you to paste the data from your spreadsheet directly into your word processing document with a dynamic link. Thus, as soon as you change the figures in the spreadsheet, you have an updated word processing file. All the major word processors and spreadsheets working under Windows support the DDE feature.

The final piece of contract magic—pasting the state's indemnification clause into the document—could be performed many ways. You could link the document to a database of clauses using the same DDE feature, or, more simply, you could create a simple macro that loads a document containing all the state clauses, seeks out the appropriate state clause, and cuts and pastes it into the document.

Behold the magic behind the automated quote system. What does it mean to you as a portable sales representative? Clearly, with the proper preparation and a little imagination, you can create just about any type of quote and dynamic contract form. Not only will this cut out the usual iterations of drafting and review, but its very timeliness will eliminate many of the usual questions that arise in the fog of elapsed time.

■ ■ ■

8

Performance Reporting

As the old saw goes, nothing gets better unless you measure it. In sales, the commission provides the incentive for measuring performance. Computers enable salespeople and managers to track sales performance in real time—no more week, month, or quarter lags. Imagine hooking your portable computer to the home office, entering your sales orders and getting instant access to your performance and commission data. Push a button and your commission funds get transferred directly into your bank account. Although this process is not yet available, this discussion looks at software you can buy and use today to measure your company's and your own performance.

Sales Performance Measurement

The basic purpose of sales performance measurement is to count the beans and pay the reps. The responsibility of sales reps on the road is usually limited to closing the deals and submitting the orders. Since each company will devise its own sales incentive system, we will not recommend specific software. In many cases, sales reps keep track of their own activity, often handled by a standard spreadsheet program, such as Lotus 1-2-3, Quattro Pro, or Excel.

Sales Performance Reporting

When it comes time to show competitive performance—one region compared to another, one sales team compared to another—charts and graphs communicate the results effectively. You can create comparative graphs with spreadsheet programs or with a dedicated graphics package such as the popular Harvard Graphics or the feature-packed Freelance Graphics for Windows. More important than which software package to use is what to chart. Let's consider some charting fundamentals.

Although it is possible to create hundreds of different charts for any set of data, most charts will be irrelevant, even confusing. Remember that the purpose of the chart is to give the reader an instant understanding of the figures. To that end, follow these tips:

1. *Establish a goal.* Ask youself: "If the viewer could see my chart for only 10 seconds, what message do I want to convey? Historical changes? Annual trends? Short-term activity?"

2. *Select the right chart type.* Programs like Harvard Graphics make it easy to present your data in a variety of forms with the click of a mouse—pie charts, bar charts, line charts, area charts, and so on. You can even combine chart forms, showing data such as historical sales data in bar form and other data such as current sales in line form. Note that each charting type has a specific purpose. The three you will use most frequently are as follows:

   Pie charts show the component parts of a whole relationship. How much did I, or my team, contribute to overall revenues? What percentage did each product line contribute to overall sales? (See Figure 8.1.)

   Bar charts compare different quantities during a specified period—sales figures for various departments or sales reps, your own sales levels for each month of the year, or your sales performance for each month for several years (a good application for a three-dimensional bar chart). (See Figure 8.2.)

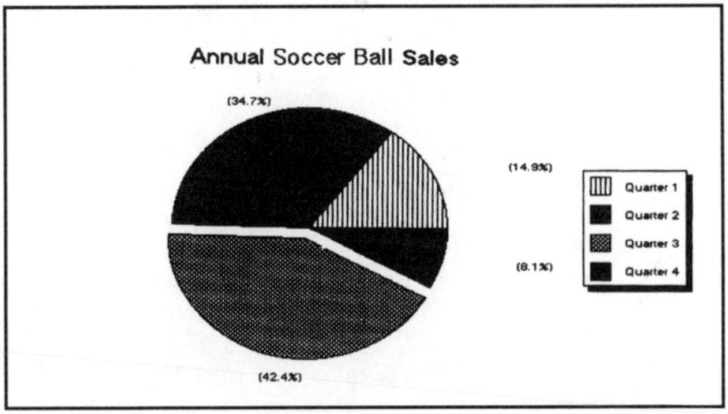

Figure 8.1 Pie charts show the component parts of a whole

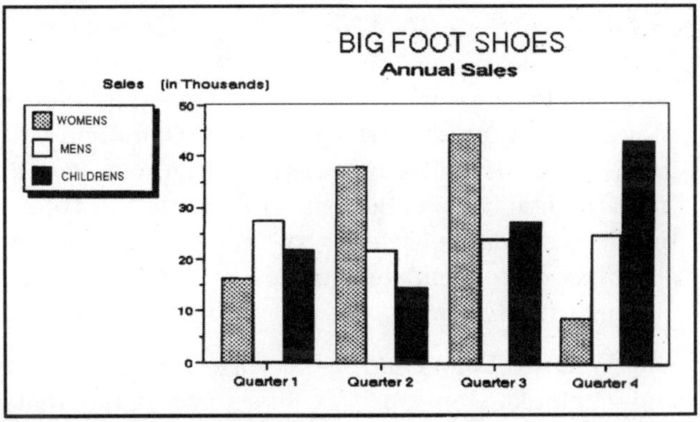

Figure 8.2 Bar charts compare different quantities over equivalent periods

Line charts show change over time, such as changes in sales from year to year, quarter to quarter, month to month, or week to week. Whereas a bar chart is static—it gives the viewer a sense of volume—a line chart is dynamic—it highlights trends. Thus, it can be effective to combine bar and line chart forms (see Figure 8.3). Use the bar portion to plot the volumes involved and the line portion to show an important trend (a new or breakaway product, a new pricing structure, etc).

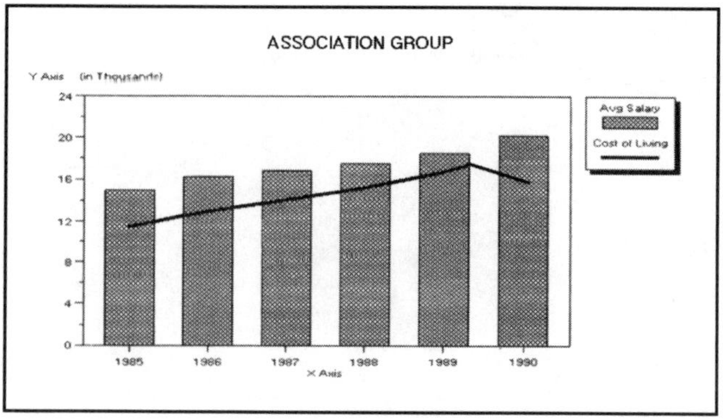

Figure 8.3 Line and bar chart combinations show both totals and trends

3. *Limit your data.* Keep the data to the minimum amount necessary to get your message across. Remember, you are not trying to show exacting detail—that is what a spreadsheet is for. Your goal is to instantly communicate a message about a trend, a changing situation, or the characteristics of a slice in time. Consolidate pie slivers, combine pencil thin bars and eliminate or consolidate unnecessary line data that might obscure the *important trends.*

4. *Limit text.* Although charting packages allow you to add text and manipulate fonts, use text judiciously. Other than titles, axis definition, legends, and critical footnotes, any text will take away from the visual impact. Administer a simple litmus test when you are tempted to add extra text. Ask yourself, "Would the chart still be instantly understandable without the extra text?" If yes, don't enter it. If no, leave it in. If in doubt, toss it out!

After you have selected the correct chart or graph type, you can enter the sales data directly into the charting program or import the sales data from your database or spreadsheet program. Many programs can create dynamic links to the underlying data—as you change the underlying sales data in your spreadsheet or database, the linked charts and graphs are automatically updated. This feature is available from all of the major graphics packages, but it is somewhat easier to implement with Windows-based software because Windows controls the linked data structure for you. In DOS-based programs such as Lotus 1-2-3 Release 3.1+, you must explicitly set up the data links.

Hardware Issues

Speed

Dedicated charting programs run better on faster computers. A video accelerator card makes a tremendous difference, especially with complex charts—waiting for the screen to redraw can interrupt your creative thought process. A high-resolution monitor makes your charting tasks easier, especially for small text used in notes and legends.

Output

As for printers, the standard laser printer is your best bet for black-and-white output. For color charts, you have a variety of options, such as Hewlett-Packard's PaintJet. Color laser printers are available, and their cost is falling dramatically, although still three to five times more expensive than basic laser printers. Color has distinct advantages for presentation since you can highlight trends, certain departments or specific sales reps. The choice depends upon presentation needs versus budget.

Portability

For the sales rep on the run, the options are more limited. As we discussed in Chapter 6, most portables are limited by their screens. Only the best backlit supertwist monochrome LCD and active matrix color displays give top-quality presentations. On the printer front, the report is even more discouraging. Although there are many good portable text printers on the market, such as the Kodak Diconix line, no printers give the same graphics output that clients have come to expect from laser printers, and no acceptable color portable printers exist. If you want to print graphics on the road, look in the yellow pages for a service bureau that will print your documents for a fee on their laser printer.

Inside Advice

1. *Use charts wisely*. It is easy to create "chart burnout" in a presentation or report. People do not want to process unlimited visual data, especially if it is redundant. Don't make performance report presentations that demonstrate your charting software's capabilities. Pick the most important data and the right charts—you will do a better job of getting your point across.
2. *Provide context*. A chart is meant to give instant understanding, but unless it is displayed in context (e.g., a report or verbal presentation), it may have no relevance to your viewers. Explain why you are showing the chart and what it means. Then let the pictures drive home your message.

■ ■ ■

9

Sales Forecasting

Sales forecasting can be performed on either the macro or the micro level. Macro forecasting involves taking the total results for the recent past and using that as a basis for extrapolating the figures into the future. Micro forecasting involves evaluating each sales prospect and projecting both the probability of successful completion and the dollar value. Both techniques produce valuable pictures of the future. Let's look at each in more detail.

Macro Forecasting

Macro forecasting is based on the assumption that the recent past is a reasonable reflection of the near future. If sales have been rising, they should continue to rise at the same rate, and vice versa. The most common technique for this type of projection is linear regression or least square line fitting, a feature present in most spreadsheet and graphing programs. Linear projections can be good estimates of the future as long as your business is not inherently cyclical or subject to radical changes in performance. Time series forecast tools capable of handling cyclical data do exist, but if your business does fluctuate, you may want to seek the advice of a qualified statistician before projecting historic data. With an unstable sales history, statistical projections may be misleading as they imply a stability that does not exist.

With these disclaimers aside, it is quite easy to make a linear projection of your sales data. For example, with Lotus 1-2-3, you enter your historic sales data into a table and invoke the /Data Regression command. You will be prompted to specify the independent (X) and dependent (Y) variables. The system will then produce a table listing the slope of the line, the Y-intercept and the "goodness of fit" (more on this later). With this data, you create the formula

```
Y-intercept + (Slope * X)
```

where X equals the length of time into the future. The result is the expected sales for the specified period. The goodness of fit value indicates how well a straight line represents the data used to calculate it. You should refer to a statistics textbook for a complete discussion of goodness of fit before relying on projected data. In addition to linear projections, it is equally easy to fit exponential, logarithmic, and other higher order curves to your data if the data warrants such a projection.

Micro Forecasting

The sales rep on the road harbors more interest in micro forecasting. In essence, this technique involves accumulating all outstanding potential sales and estimating two values: the probability of closing the sale and the expected total dollar value of the sale. The product of these two figures (Closure Percent * Dollar Value) yields the expected value of the sale. As the probability of closure nears 100 percent (1.0), the expected value will approach the total sale value. If you add up the individual expected values, you will get the total expected sales for the period.

An accurate representation of each sale value and expected closure rate is the key to the success of micro forecasting. Each sales rep is responsible for forecasting his or her own activity. Many of the integrated sales automation tools discussed in Chapter 6 contain utilities to facilitate individual estimates and consolidations on a branch, regional, or corporate level.

The major risk of expected value calculations is the tendency to be overly optimistic about the closure rates and failing to update the rate as the deal waxes and wanes. Individual sales reps also tend to pick benchmark probabilities that they apply to outcomes of high, medium, and low expectations. If the various sales reps use differing benchmarks, they will consistently forecast differently on a relative scale.

By periodically comparing past forecasts to actual results, a sales rep can refine his or her estimation techniques. If he or she constantly overestimates, he or she can be taught to be more realistic. Alternatively, a comparison can be used to modify the estimates of that sales rep on a "behind the scenes basis" before adding them into the total forecast, as it is often easier to modify errors of estimates on a gross basis than on an individual transaction basis.

After you have created a sales forecast, what can you do with it? It can be used to measure actual performance against the initial estimate for a post-period analysis. More importantly, it can be used to measure performance on a real-time basis. By constantly refining your closure probability estimates during the current period, you can determine day to day whether you are above, below, or on target for the period. Duplicating what we naturally do when we evaluate our performance, the sales automation tool organizes the process and allows us to be more precise.

■ ■ ■

Creating Sales Material

With the advent of personal computers and inexpensive desktop publishing or high-performance word processing software, the salesperson in the trenches has the ability to create his or her own professional sales material. Be warned, however, that with power also comes risk and responsibility. It is easy to get caught up in the features and lose sight of the sales communication objectives. Although a discussion of graphic design and copywriting is beyond the scope of this chapter, it is nonetheless helpful to know what constitutes good sales literature and how you can create it with off-the-shelf software and hardware. By knowing the elements of good sales literature, you can create prototypes that your company's design and production staff can use to develop finished pieces.

The ABCs of Sales Brochures

Too many sales brochures end up in the trashcan because the people who create them fail to understand the real purpose of a sales brochure—to educate customers. Instead, companies try to create "mood pieces" that have nothing to do with the product or service. Even Fortune 500 companies make the mistake of selling image rather than substance, and ultimately that mistake comes home to roost at the cash register. Whether you are a one-person company; you are responsible for developing sales brochures; or you are a representative of a large sales team, you should insist that your company's sales brochures do the following:

- Educate customers.
- Create a compelling "sales environment"—in other words, present your products and services in a way that attracts.
- Differentiate your company from the competition so that you stand out as the vendor of choice.
- Demonstrate how your company's products and services solve problems, improve efficiency, or reduce costs.
- Position your products and services in the competitive arena.
- Let customers tell their own stories—nothing convinces more than testimony from satisfied customers.

Your company's sales brochures should avoid the following:

- Pictures of the president and "executive platitudes"—all that does is bloat executive egos. Customers don't care.
- Cryptic teasers. Clever and enticing copy may be a plus, but if the customer or prospect does not "get it" within a very short time, he or she will not "buy it" either.
- Competitor bashing. Your product must stand on its own. Although you want to differentiate it from competing products, focus primarily on your strengths.

Collateral Literature

In addition to your regular sales brochures, you may need ancillary pieces to support new product launches, to provide detailed technical specifications of certain products and services, and to inform customers and prospects about the full breadth of your company's products and services. You can use a computer to create the following types of collateral literature:

Specification sheets and technical bulletins. Suppose that you are on the road and need to develop a focused spec sheet for a client that you are visiting the next day. With your portable PC, standard word processor, and portable bubble jet printer, you can accomplish this easily. Just keep in mind the goal of this type of literature—clarity.

Keep the text and design focused on explaining how your products work. Avoid competitive posturing, as a specification sheet is strictly for conveying "unbiased" information.

Price sheets. Price sheets are ideal candidates for desktop publishing, especially if they involve numbers that frequently change. Make the price sheet easy-to-read and legible. Reduce the total number of offerings to the items holding particular interest for the client. With page-layout software and a portable computer, you can maintain a fully formatted version of the entire price sheet and extract only those portions required for the particular client. In this way, you are able to create a custom price quote with very little time or effort.

If you bring a portable printer or can borrow your client's, you can create a formal price quote or full proposal on the fly, print the proposal on site and get the client's signature on the dotted line. You will experience fewer delays, fewer opportunities for second thoughts, and fewer expressions of "I'll get back to you."

Newsletters. Newsletters can be excellent marketing and sales tools if done properly. They maintain contact with existing customers and show prospects that your company does more than push products—it is out there with innovative ideas and on-going support.

An entire book is needed to adequately explain the basics of good newsletter writing/production, but a few tips are worth mentioning:

- Do not use the newsletter as an "ad rag." If it contains substantive information (e.g. insights into new regulations, new ways to use products for increased efficiency, etc.), people will read it.
- Avoid hollow messages from the president—customers do not care.
- Use the newsletter to share information such as insights from customers and your company's technical support people, upcoming conferences, etc.
- Encourage reader participation with a "forum"—accept letters and provide responses.

- Keep the newsletter short and easy to read; the idea is for the customer or prospect to quickly browse through the piece and pass it on. Run numerous short articles rather than two or three lengthy features. The ultimate measure of success is feedback from a customer who clips an article and says, "This is just what we needed to hear."
- Maintain a thorough database of current customers, past customers, and prospects and make sure that they all get the newsletter. This may seem obvious, but many salespeople are frustrated because important people are not on the mailing list. If you are using an integrated sales automation system, each sales rep can be responsible for maintaining his or her own database of customers and prospects. When it is time to prepare a mailing, the lists can be merged, purged of duplicates, and used to create the master mailing list.

When you have your ideas for copy and graphic treatment for brochures and other sales literature, you have a wealth of software options at your disposal. In fact, word processing and desktop publishing represent the most fully developed and robust area of microcomputing today. Let's take a look at some of your options.

Selecting the Right Type of Software Program

The first choice you have to make is whether you are going to use a word processor or desktop publishing program. The two are very different, despite ads claiming that you can "have it all" in one program. Word processors are designed to get the words on paper with a minimum of fuss and features. Desktop publishing (DTP) packages are page layout workhorses that provide extreme flexibility in design, font control, spacing, and other layout considerations but at a cost of much slower speeds and more complicated operation.

Many of today's word processors have desktop publishing capabilities. Word processors designed for DOS are generally only useful for very simple jobs, because you can only see what you're going to print by shifting into a print "preview" mode. This is clumsy and makes creating a page layout a laborious task. Word processors that operate under Windows are more useful for desktop publishing tasks because they offer full-time "WYSIWYG" (what-you-see-is-what-you-get) displays. Rather than guessing at what the finished product will look like, you'll see it on screen and have a much better sense of what to do next. Word for Windows, WordPerfect for Windows, and Ami Pro are several leading contenders for Windows word processors with advanced layout capabilities.

On the desktop publishing side, the current leading desktop publishing programs (Quark, PageMaker, Ventura) have considerably more text creation and editing capabilities than their predecessors. Even so, you would not want to input the text for a lengthy sales brochure with a desktop publishing program. Except for entering small bits of text, use a word processor to create and edit your copy. Desktop publishing programs do not have the kind of important editing features or speed that you are probably accustomed to in full-powered word processing programs. Only after you are satisfied with your text should you import it into a DTP program for layout and printing.

For serious design and layout work, use a desktop publisher. Although Windows-based word processors offer impressive capabilities, they do not provide the kind of exacting typographic and page composition control that desktop publishing programs offer. Desktop publishers also provide better control over graphic elements, making it easy to place and size photographs, charts, and graphs into your text.

Use the following guidelines for deciding between the two types of programs:

Word processors with Desktop Publishing Capabilities
Bulletins, fliers, and ads
Announcements and invitations
Price lists

continues

Desktop publishers
Multipage sales brochures
Multicolumn newsletters
Documents with numerous graphic elements (graphics files, halftones, etc.)
Documents with multiple colors that will require color separations for the printer

If it seems confusing or redundant to use both a word processor and a desktop publisher to create your sales literature, be assured that it is. Fortunately, this area of software is highly competitive, and the publishers of word processing and desktop publishing programs are vying to create the one product that truly does it all. Currently, Windows-based word processors have remarkable capabilities to combine text and graphics, and each update provides continuing desktop publishing power. Thus, Ami Pro or Word for Windows may be quite adequate for your needs.

If you are already using a word processing program, another option is to purchase a low-end desktop publishing package such as Microsoft's Publisher or Power Up Software's Express Publisher. Both are relatively inexpensive and may be exactly what you need to create your sales materials. If you find that you need more capabilities, you can graduate to Quark, PageMaker, Ventura or one of the other high-end packages.

Choosing the Right Hardware

Computers

The more page composition, layout, and design you want to do yourself, the more horsepower you are going to need. Graphics applications are among the most CPU-intensive. To do serious work, you will want a computer with these minimum specifications:

- 386, 20-Mhz processor (CPU)
- 2 megabytes RAM

- 100 megabyte hard disk (DTP files are huge, and graphics files are even bigger. A single page with a few graphics can exceed 1 megabyte.)
- 14-inch VGA color monitor

Preferably, you'll use the following:

- 486 processor
- 4 megabytes or more RAM
- 200 megabyte hard disk
- Graphics coprocessor video card
- 17-inch SVGA (super VGA) color monitor

The last two items are particularly important. A graphics accelerator card, such as the Diamond Stealth board, can make a dramatic improvement in the speed of screen redraw. The larger color monitor will enable you to see a full page with legible type rather than scroll around the document. Be aware that your hard disk can never be too large if you plan to store graphic images and many fonts—both consume enormous amounts of disk space.

Printers—The Laser Connection

The final element to consider is your printer, and the advice is simple: laser. To create any kind of effective sales literature, you will need a laser printer. Dot matrix simply looks amateurish. For simple sales pieces, the resolution (300 dots per inch—"dpi") of a standard laser printer is fine. The Hewlett-Packard Series III LaserJets offer "resolution-enhancement technology" that makes 300-dpi type appear to be closer to 600-dpi, and IBM, as well as several other laser printer makers, now offer true 600-dpi printers. For high-end sales pieces that will be produced by a commercial printer, you will first want to have your files output on a Linotronic or Varityper imagesetter. Linotronic imagesetters offer resolutions of up to 2,540 dots per inch. Many printers, as well as the growing number of desktop publishing "boutiques" that have sprung up around the country, can handle your Linotronic needs.

If you are on the road, do not despair. You can use those lonely nights to create your masterpieces and have the local printers print and reproduce them. Most major cities have one or more DTP "boutiques" where you can rent by the hour a PC and your favorite DTP software. Many even have high-resolution printing options and fast turnaround offset printing available.

Inside Advice

- *Use the technology sparingly.* When it comes to sales literature, less is often more. Do not go hog-wild with fonts—in general, placing more than two different font families on a page will create chaos. Also, you do not have to import 10 different pictures on each page just because your page layout software can.
- *Remember that the medium is not the message.* Although the visual appeal certainly plays a large role in whether your sales literature will be read, ultimately you must create an effective message.
- *Take the "nanosecond test."* Ask yourself: "Does my literature lose the reader for a nanosecond?" If so, your literature will wind up in the circular file. Remember, people are bombarded with information every day, and their chief impulse is to reduce the burden. Thus, they are looking for excuses *not* to read your (or anyone else's) sales literature. Give them a reason to keep reading, and you will be that much closer to making a sale.

■ ■ ■

Making the Connection: Modems

Communicating via microcomputers is essential for today's traveling salesperson—telecommunications opens the door to E-mail, instant order transmittal, and a host of other valuable actions. It can also open the door to migraine headaches—data communications is the least standardized of all microcomputing functions. It is subject to the variabilities in telephone line, microwave, fiber-optic, and satellite connections. Fortunately, if you know the tricks of the trade and have a bit of patience, you will be able to transmit and receive information with a minimum of frustration.

Communications Hardware

The Modem

The first item you need for data communications is a modem (which stands for MOdulation/DEModulation). A modem converts, or modulates, your computer's digital signal into an analog signal that your telephone lines use. The modem then converts, or demodulates, the signal back into digital form so that the receiving modem can interpret it. The majority of modems conform to the "Hayes" standard—specifications found in modems manufactured by Hayes Microcomputer Products, Inc. The main considerations in choosing a modem are Hayes compatibility, speed, and price.

Today, 2,400 baud (data transmittal at approximately 2,400 characters per second) is the standard, and modems operating at that speed can be purchased for $100 or less. Faster modems are also available—9,600 baud and higher, but for a price. The advantage of speed is that it takes less time to transmit data and, therefore, costs you less in long-distance calls. The disadvantage of speed is that the faster the transmission speed, the more the communication is prone to problems because of poor telephone connections.

Laptop users have the following decision: purchase an internal modem or an external "pocket size" modem. This issue is covered in depth in *Portable Communications*, by Michael A. Banks (Brady, 1991). We will discuss a few key considerations here. With an internal modem, you do not have to carry around a modem or a cable. Even though external modems are small and light, they still represent one more item to account for when you are rushing between City A and City B. In addition, you will need a steady supply of batteries to feed your external modem—they eat the batteries like candy. On the other hand, internal modems from the manufacturer of your computer tend to be very expensive, although third-party vendors, such as Holmes and Megahertz, offer internal models for the more popular laptops and notebooks.

If you have an internal modem, make sure that you do not power it on unless you're actively transmitting or receiving data—internal modems are a significant drain on your computer's battery. Each laptop maker has a specific command or function for turning the modem on and off.

Accessories

You may need hardware in addition to the modem to communicate with your home office for mail, for order submittal, etc. Always have an RJ-11 (standard) telephone cord with you while on the road. Most modern or renovated hotels have telephone jacks or modular telephones that you can disconnect and hook up to your modem. Some hotels also have "dataports"—essentially a spare RJ-11 jack that enables you to plug in your modem without disconnecting the telephone.

But what if your motel or hotel does not have modular telephones? You have several options:

- A new device, called a direct connect handset adaptor, makes it easy to carry out data communication. It taps in between the plug on the handset and the plug on the base of the telephone. (Only the most antiquated single-line telephones have hardwired handsets.) Two examples of the direct connect adapter are Konexx by Unlimited Systems and CP+ Connection II by CP+.

- Originally, modem transmission was done via rubber cups that fit over the ear and mouth pieces of the handset. The coupler (essentially a speaker and a microphone attached to the mouthpiece and the earpiece, respectively) converted the electronic signal of the modem into audible signals that could be directly fed into a standard telephone handset and vice versa. You can purchase acoustic couplers through Traveling Software—allowing you to communicate from pay telephones, multi-line telephone systems, and very old single-line telephones.

- Another variation for connecting with a recalcitrant telephone involves removing the mouthpiece and connecting directly to its contacts in the handset. One such system is sold by Travelling Software under the name "Blackjack."

- If all else fails, you can resort to guerilla telephone tapping techniques. The easiest way to approach this situation is to buy a complete kit of prefabricated telephone tools such as Tele-Toolkit by CP+. The kit contains "alligator" clips connected to a standard plug as well as other useful tools and, most importantly, a complete set of instructions for safely attacking the innards of your hotel telephone. You take apart the telephone or the jack and place the clips over the appropriate wires as explained in the booklet included with the kit. This is not difficult, but you will want to know what you are doing before you start.

The Cellular Connection

Like so many technologies that once sounded futuristic, cellular modems are here. The advantage, of course, is that you can transmit data in any area in which you can make a cellular call, eliminating the need for telephone hookups. If you already own a cellular telephone, you may have to purchase an adapter to connect your modem. Some recent cellular telephone models come with a modem connection built in.

Several portable PCs, including models offered by AT&T, NCR, and NEC, are equipped with built-in cellular modems and E-mail software.

Another approach is offered by Motorola, called EMBARC. This wireless messaging system entails a cellular device that attaches to your laptop or palmtop and allows users to send E-mail and tap into various news services. You can also send E-mail messages to multiple receivers with a few keystrokes

Communications Software

Today, you can choose from scores of communication packages, and it would require a full-length book to explain their features, virtues, etc. However, the traveling salesperson should use the least memory-hungry program he or she can find. You probably do not need a lot of bells and whistles to communicate with your home base or to send an E-mail communication via MCI mail. A basic program such as Crosstalk XVI or ProComm will do. Make sure that the software has the communication protocols you need to transfer files. Also, choose a program that can be customized for an LCD display—if you cannot see the program, you will be shooting in the dark.

Cutting Communications Costs

Two factors affect the cost of a communication: the length of the communication and the time you place the call. You have considerably more control over the former than the latter. With a busy schedule, you may not be able to call at the optimal hours, or you may be too tired to stay up until very low, late-night rates apply.

Fortunately, you can control the length of the transmission by using a high-speed modem or compressing your data with a program such as ARC or PKZIP by PKWARE, Inc. Programs like ARC and PKZIP can crunch text files by as much as 90 percent, depending on the application, and with smaller files, less time is needed to transmit them. The programs also allow you to combine multiple files into one single file for transmission; thus, you do not have to reissue separate send commands for each file. When the other party receives your file, he or she simply "expands" (for ARC) or "unzips" (for PKZIP) the file, and the files are restored to full size.

On the Road: Putting Your Communications Capabilities to Work

Before taking off with laptop in hand, we strongly recommend that you try some local communications, preferably in the same room with the receiving computer. You can iron out any kinks, and you greatly reduce the chances of finding yourself in a situation in which you cannot send or receive important data.

Assuming that you are up and running, the following are suggestions for improving your sales effectiveness with a modem:

- *Transmit sales information back to the home office*. This can be an important way to gain a competitive edge through highly responsive customer service. Fax/modems (see Chapter 12) can also be very effective in this regard. Depending on your order entry system, you will transmit the information in database, spreadsheet, or word processing form. For simple orders, you could send an E-mail letter through MCI. Another approach is to send batches of orders via modem at the end of each day.

- *Make literature requests.* It is important to send additional literature, quotes, estimates, etc. as soon as possible so that current customers and prospects know that your company considers them a priority. Quick turnaround also reflects your commitment to superior customer service, which is essential to gaining a competitive advantage. You can use a modem to transmit requests for samples, quotes, etc. as often as necessary. When you are dashing from appointment to appointment, it may be impractical to telephone in your requests, but if you can find a few moments in your car or on the plane or train to amalgamate requests into one communication, you will offer your prospects and customers quick turnaround while boosting your own efficiency.

Inside Advice

- *Keep it simple.* Less is generally more when it comes to telecommunications. If you are a busy salesperson, you will want to limit your software knowledge to transmitting files and sending E-mail, not to figuring out how to write fancy script files. Select software that you can use immediately or with minimal experimenting and training.

- *Build familiarity with your equipment before you hit the road.* The time to make an escape plan is before you need it. That line of thinking applies to communications gear as well. As we stressed earlier, make connections locally *before* you need them, or you may find yourself in a frustrating situation.

- *Do not forsake conventional communication methods.* You can gain significant efficiencies by incorporating laptop communications into your sales life, but do not hesitate to pick up the telephone and convey information to your home office when appropriate. The effective salesperson combines the best technologies with common sense to get the job done.

■ ■ ■

12

Making the Connection: Faxing

The facsimile (fax) machine has become an essential tool for business people in general, sales people in particular. The good news is that you can take your fax with you inside your computer—wherever you go. (If you have a non fax/modem, you can still fax through MCI and other services.) In Chapter 11, we gave you a brief course in modem communications. Here, we will focus on opportunities for faxing from the road.

About Fax/Modems

Today, many portable and internal modems are available with built-in fax circuitry. Thus, you can create a document in your word processor, and, instead of transmitting it to another modem, you can transmit it to any fax machine. In a sense, you are using someone else's fax as your printer and the telephone line as a very long cable.

You have several choices in fax/modems. Some offer send-only capabilities and generally cost less than send-receive modems. Some offer send capabilities at 9,600 baud but receive capabilities at 4,800 baud, and some offer 9,600 baud send/receive capabilities. Choosing the type of modem depends on your situation. If you are going to be only faxing orders from your computer, then send-only will be sufficient. If you plan to use your machine to receive important information from your home office via fax, receive capabilities will be important.

One limiting factor on the receiving end concerns output. Until recently, the only way to see an incoming fax was to view it on-screen in graphics mode or to print it out. The former required a laptop with a high-quality screen; the latter required toting around or finding a printer. A new twist on receiving faxes has been developed by Calera, called FAX/GRABBER. This software performs the equivalent of optical character recognition (OCR) on the incoming fax and then converts it into a format that you can use with a word processor. Although this sounds intriguing and promising, bear in mind that like OCR, the translation will not be perfect, and you may miss some information. Even so, it offers an alternate means of getting information from your company's or client's fax machine into your word processor.

Sending Faxes from Your Laptop

You are now ready to fax in an order from the road. What will it look like when printed on your client's fax machine? That depends on whether you are a DOS or Windows user. With DOS-based faxing, you create a word processed document or a spreadsheet, and you either convert it to ASCII or create it for output to an Epson or other standard dot-matrix printer. Some fax software will let you send faxes directly from your application; others require you to exit and switch to a separate program. Either way, what you fax may not look exactly like what you have on the screen. The fonts may be crude depending on the emulation capability of the fax board and the software you're using. If you are sending faxes to your home office, quality may not be an issue. If you are sending faxes to a client or customer, however, you may want to consider other options. Also, unless you scan in your company's letterhead, everything you fax will appear as text on blank paper.

Here is where Windows truly shines. With Windows fax applications, such as WinFax Pro by Delrina, what you see is what you fax—any font, any graphic. You install your fax/modem as a Windows print driver and select it from the Print menu when you are ready to fax. You can scan in or create a letterhead, use whatever fonts are available to you in Windows, and include lines and boxes—whatever is on-screen will come out on the receiving fax. In addition, by selecting the high-resolution mode, the received fax may actually be superior to one sent by a conventional fax machine with an optical scanner.

The downside is that using Windows on the road requires a laptop with a lot of horsepower—a 386-20 Mhz laptop, at least 4 megabytes of RAM, a sizable hard disk (at least 60 megabytes), a *superb* screen, and a pointing device. If you have the hardware, Windows is the way to go.

Making Connections

Connecting your laptop to a fax machine is the same as connecting it to a modem—all of the issues are the same as those described in Chapter 11.

Cutting Fax Costs

Like any kind of data transmission, the cost depends on the length of time needed to complete the fax and the time of day. Send your faxes at the most economical hours and keep them as brief as possible to reduce costs.

Three simple things you can do to slim your fax bill:

1. Eliminate cover sheets whenever possible.
2. Single space all documents unless spacing is critical.
3. Look for single words or sentences that flow onto the next page and then change your margins or do a quick edit to the page.

The MCI Alternative

For occasional faxes, you may want to use a service such as that provided by MCI. The idea is simple—you modem a text file to MCI, and MCI will fax it to whomever you like. If the recipient's fax line is busy, MCI will keep trying until the fax gets through. If you encounter a busy signal with your laptop, you may have to leave your machine hooked up for hours. Call MCI to learn about fax capabilities.

Putting Your Mobile Fax Capability To Work

What can you fax from your computer? Here are a few suggestions:

- Customer orders
- Literature requests
- Requests for estimates and quotes
- New prospects to be added to your company's mailing lists
- Competitive information/requests for competitive research

Inside Advice

Do not get caught up in technology. Although there are many good reasons to send information from your computer to a fax machine, you can also waste a lot of time and money doing so. Use common sense to determine whether or not your transmission warrants the time and cost of electronic transmission. Also, beware of "faxlash"—many customers are annoyed by unnecessary faxes.

■ ■ ■

13

Case Study 1

An Integrated Sales Support Software System

In the following case study, we explore the issues that arise when Alpha Dental Company, a midsize national dental supply company, confronts the collision within their independently developed, "built-at-home" sales tool and seeks to find an integrated software solution. We will consider the selection of an integrated sales support software package, one containing all of the functions needed to support the day-to-day efforts of a sales representative without overlap and double data entry.

This case study highlights the dilemma faced by all companies at some point in their growth—when incrementally improving the status quo is not enough and discovering the need to make a clean break and find a total solution is imperative. We will discuss the objections, the issues that came up during the selection process (costs, benefits, training, and support), the forces of resistance, the actual implementation process, and the end result.

The Business Problem

In a normal business day, each of us comes to recognize the power of personal computing. Only recently have the functions of the sales representative been considered in the corporate automation process. The Alpha Dental Company is no exception. Alpha Dental sells its leading dental probe products with the aid of 250 sales representatives divided into six sales regions nationwide. Plans to expand internationally are underway.

National headquarters are located in Morristown, New Jersey, and the manufacturing and inventorying of products are housed in St. Louis, Missouri. The six regional offices are located in Chicago, San Francisco, St. Louis, Houston, Atlanta, and New York. St. Louis was chosen as the inventory storage location because of its central location to most accounts. Telecommunication connections between offices is rudimentary.

First, we will meet the players in this drama: a group of talented and well-intentioned professionals. We will focus on the significant actions of Tom Smith, the "PC-tinkering" sales representative; Sally Jones, the self-starting Information Systems Group programmer/analyst; Ben Bradford, the frustrated regional sales manager; Dick Cranston, the communication-conscious president; and Jan Clatchy, an account service representative, also known as "the file drawer foot dragger."

In the normal course of Alpha Dental's business, the Information Systems Group (ISG) spent significant amounts of time managing post-sale reporting—providing to management the data detailing sales and related expenses—basically "what was going on" and "where the company had been." As we shall see, some of the people in the company began thinking about using computers to drive the future—a proactive approach to computing rather than a system of historical reflection, controlling versus reporting, looking forward and not just behind.

Historically, as companies began investigating the power of personal computing, they first implemented word processing and spreadsheet functions into the organization. Secretaries and accountants were the first to obtain computing tools that allowed them to do their jobs more productively. Computer-literate sales people began using these same tools to help support their own selling efforts. They selected the accountant's database programs to develop client lists and the secretary's word processor for writing client correspondence and designing sales presentations. They chose spreadsheet programs for creating simplified expense reports and commission calculators. Then, the inevitable happened: someone decided there must be a "better way" and designed a software program specifically for the sales person.

Tom Smith, sales representative for Alpha Dental, decided to practice some of the programming tricks he learned from his college computer course. At nights and on the weekends, he began creating a software program for increasing his client contact management. Though not the highest selling sales representative, Tom was always known as a resourceful rep, bringing many ideas to the solution of a problem. His current self-appointed task, the creation of a software sales system, was no exception. While leaning back in his chair with his arms folded across his chest, he envisioned building a strategic selling system that could help him deliver proposals and close deals in the same way a stealth bomber could penetrate enemy radar and deliver its payload. If done properly, he knew his stealth sales system could increase his income and prestige within Alpha Dental. He would even share his resulting software with other sales representatives from his division. The development of his home-grown stealth sales system became a pass-the-time activity that gave him great delight.

Tom Smith's stealth sales system consisted of a general-purpose database program adapted to track account numbers and call dates. Tom took great care to put in information that he wanted to collect about his clients. In addition to their names, addresses, telephone numbers, and account numbers, he tracked the names of their spouses and the names and birthdays of their children. By increasing his birthday card mailings, Tom's name would be kept current in his customers' minds. To provide better client rapport, he even designed into his system the additional fields necessary for tracking clubs and social activity preferences, including preferences for restaurants and sporting events. With a special software utility program, he added a "macro" feature that automatically filled in some of this information on the screen by pressing a single key. He added colors to the screen to highlight certain fields and even made the screen flash the name STEALTH followed by an audible "ka-boom" to give his software users the feeling that this software had some punch. He picked up these software graphic and audio enhancement features free as shareware from a bulletin board service. Thus, it did not cost him or the company anything to add these slick features to the program.

Tom's sales tasks consisted of making personal visits to resellers, dentist offices, and health clinics who purchased Alpha Dental's dental probes and other dental supplies. He made two appointments a day—one in the morning and the other in the afternoon. Usually, between appointments, he took a client to lunch to talk about new products and their features. After returning from these sales calls, he entered the outcome of the meetings into his newly designed Stealth sales system on his desktop personal computer. He wished he could convince his manager to buy him a new portable notebook computer, so he could perform this data-entry work minute by minute rather than at the end of a long day.

Meanwhile, back in the Information Systems Group, programmer/analyst Sally Jones was developing a comprehensive sales reporting system that would collect sales data from each region, consolidate it, and report the individual, regional, and company-wide performance for the previous month. As a dedicated programmer, she labored evenings and weekends to create the best, most responsive sales reporting system possible. She nicknamed it IRIS for Integrated Reporting Information System and for her love of flowers and gardening. She thought of her job as that of a historian—one who could collect information about historical transactions and present the information in a way that would let any reader know what the company had done. As we shall see, Sally was becoming an expert in creating the documents that described the history of Alpha Dental and unveiling where they had been. Sally became the champion of historical sales reporting.

Ben Bradley, a senior company man and western regional sales manager, was known for bringing home the bacon. He had collected good sales representatives, trained them well, and motivated them with incentives. However, Ben had lost three sales representatives in the last three months, and this turnover was killing his regional sales performance. One day, Ben had a brainstorm: "If I could get all my sales people to enter their sales leads into a single computer in the secretary's office, I could ensure more continuity in sales." He knew that every time a sales representative left, Ben lost continuity with that rep's clients. Ben lost the names and addresses, the history of the contact, and the next actions to be taken on the account.

Ben Bradford was joining the computer age and subscribed to *PC Novice Magazine* (Peed Corporation, 800-848-1478) and *Mobile Office Magazine* (CurtCo Publishing, 818-593-6100) to learn more about software and hardware. He became aware of manual methods and their electronic or computer counterparts. Even though his sales reps had created manual card files, the information was never available when or where it was needed. He wanted to take advantage of the powerful look-up and sorting features of a computer. Further, he recognized that leads and prospects were not getting follow-through and that he had no way of tracking them or the sales representative's activity on them. He thought a computer database could help.

Even Alpha Dental's president, Dick Cranston, got into the act of bringing new technology to the sales force. He was intrigued with a product he saw advertised in his boating magazine—an infrared signaling device that sends information from location to location without the need of telephone lines. Because he recognized the value of his ship-to-shore telephone connection, he was curious about ways he could help his sales force communicate more efficiently and thereby increase sales. He called together a presidential task force to study "sales representative communication."

Forces of Resistance

Change is difficult. Some people are born to stifle it while others are addicted to continuous change. Fortunately, for most organizations, the tendency of resistance to change is also a force for stability and growth. Jan Clatchy is the force for stability and nonchange at Alpha Dental. As an account service representative, her job is to ensure the smooth flow of information back and forth between clients and Alpha Dental. She documents any errors on *Form 2A. Shipping Deviation Report* that may have occurred in shipping Alpha Dental orders. This form tracks a sale through the Alpha Dental Company until, on the desk of the shipping clerk, it is stamped "shipped" and is returned to Jan's desk. From here, it is filed in her "completed tasks" file next to her desk. This is the file Jan developed over the last 14 years as the final resting place for all important documents—each one color coded, alphabetically cross-referenced, and very well organized.

Similarly, on *Form J4. Customer Complaint Form*, Jan Clatchy enters the names, addresses, and account numbers of buyers that provide either written or verbal complaints to Alpha Dental. The Customer Complaint Form is feared by all on whose desk it lands because it gets senior level attention. Heads roll if too many forms pile up on any one desk. Jan enjoys most the task of pushing this form. This single form enables her to bring together all the forces of the company to solve a problem. Sometimes, she can even call the president of Alpha Dental, Dick Cranston, get his attention, and cause him to act. In all cases, the *J4. Customer Complaint Form* must be signed by the president and kept in the file at Jan's desk following final resolution.

Someone once made the mistake of explaining to Jan that the new sales and marketing automation project would make all forms obsolete. As Jan heard it, no longer would there be a need for files, file cabinets, or color coding. "How silly can they be," she thought. "No one will ever replace my filing system . . . it is perfect, and I have spent years creating it!"

The Problem Grows

After reading about the many well-intentioned initiatives in the previous section, you may conclude that soon all the separate computerization initiatives are about to collide. You are correct.

As each of these welcome initiatives took on more momentum, they also emboldened their champions to demand more—more company resources to support each person's pet project, more people to use each system, more time and money to develop each concept further, more time and money for training, and more people to be trained to use each person's systems and tools. The president's need for "better communication," the regional manager's need for "turnover risk reduction," the sales representative's need for "a Stealth sales system," and the programmer/analyst's need for a "comprehensive sales reporting system" all led to a collision of ideas, territories, initiatives, and financial resources. In short, they were caught in a log-jam of good intentions.

(P.S. Every time Jan Clatchy, account service representative and keeper of the files, received a routing memo regarding the computerization project, she held it on her desk for a few extra days to slow it down in the routing process. Sometimes, she even inadvertently filed it, thus taking it out of circulation. It was petty, she knew, but somehow she felt it was the right thing to do. "They may possibly come to their senses soon," she thought. "Then my files will be safe.")

The Boiling Point

Things came to a head at an annual budget meeting when all the players were proposing to increase the scale and scope of their respective projects. The Stealth software crew wanted notebook computers issued to all sales reps at the next sales meeting. (Although no one yet had figured out why the STEALTH message followed by the audio kaboom caused all the test notebook computers to fail on program start-up, some thought it could be traced to the shareware program design, but nobody had the time or requisite programming knowledge to track it down.) The programmer/analyst from the Information Systems Group wanted a wide area network installed to link all offices. The president's task force on communication wanted voice activated pagers for voice transmission. The regional manager wanted to hire a database programming company to design a corporate-wide database for prospect tracking. Total cost for implementing all these independent and overlapping efforts, including hardware, software, training, and support, was astronomical. The president decided then and there that an integrated approach to the sales representative computerization program had to be developed.

Dilemma Resolution

A second presidential task force was created to develop an integrated approach to sales representative computerization. A leader was chosen, and people from each of the various interest groups were invited to participate. In order to participate in the group, they had to commit to being open to all solutions and not lobbying for their own pet projects.

The first meeting of the Presidential Task Force on Sales Representative Computerization (PTFSRC) included a request to define the objectives of the group. Their objectives were reduced to six fundamental goals:

1. Increased sales representative productivity
2. Increased customer satisfaction
3. Increased reporting speed and capability
4. Increased company profitability
5. Controlling versus reporting—looking forward
6. Reduced cost of operation

Difficulties To Overcome

Fortunately, each of the members of the Presidential Task Force on Sales Representative Computerization was a lucid speaker and good committee member. They met twice per week, set goals for each meeting, and conducted brainstorming and idea-generating meetings. They even explored possible sticking points in the operation of their committee and its future recommendations. For example, they created a list of difficulties they needed to consider:

1. Conflicts of interest were present among the committee participants.
2. The president was personally involved with his own project.
3. "Not Invented Here" syndrome was a problem for some.
4. Redundant data entry had to be curtailed.
5. The high cost of sales representatives turnover had to be addressed.
6. Projected costs of following all paths were astronomical.

The project gained new momentum on the day the president got an angry call from a big client. The client was disappointed with the lack of account follow-through and wondered if anyone at Alpha Dental cared about his needs and his account. The president assured the client that the client would get greater attention in the future. However, the president had no way to reach the appointed sales representative nor to investigate the current level of account support. "If only I could have seen all the information about this account here in my office, I might have been able to help," exclaimed the president. "I need to be able to communicate quickly and efficiently with our sales force . . . this sales computer system project has got to go faster!" Unfortunately for Alpha Dental, the grumpy client took his business to another dental supply vendor, including a significant amount of sales revenue.

The Solution Process

The committee divided into selected work groups, and each was responsible for researching various aspects of a sales computerization project. The most important task was the selection of an integrated software package that was widely available and that met all the objectives of the project.

The committee considered conventional integrated software packages that connected word processing, database management, and spreadsheets into a single comprehensive program. They considered custom-designed specialized software, wrote Requests for Proposals (RFPs) to software design companies, and got price and schedule quotes for these custom programming jobs. The one-year lag time associated with newly created software was unacceptably long. The team wanted to move ahead. After reviewing all the cost/benefit considerations, they selected Sales Ally from Scherrer Resources, Inc., an off-the-shelf integrated package specifically designed for supporting sales and marketing tasks.

Alpha Dental's team created a systematic plan of attack for both the software selection and implementation which included a project survey, design specification, hardware and software vendor selection, documentation development, service selection, and procurement. Additionally, they ensured that the project had a testing program, a training process, hot-line support, and a performance evaluation. Let's look at each step in detail.

1. *Project survey.* The project survey, or needs analysis, formed the basis of the project design specification. The survey consisted of a review of the following topics: hardware, account management, sales and management reports, data and information distribution, electronic mail and computer access, and other sales support software. In addition, they considered currently available Alpha Dental resources, consultants, system integrators, responsibilities, schedules, budgets, and management commitment. Third, and very importantly, they had to create a portable system that could travel with the sales representatives instead of binding them to their desks. The system had to be mobile and adaptable to the reps' on-the-go work styles.

2. *Design specification.* The design specification was a written document that defined the characteristics of the hardware, software, and services to be provided. With the project survey as input, the overall design specification was created in outline format. Each element was further detailed by the chosen responsible person. The completion of the fully developed design specification represented a significant milestone in the Alpha Dental sales automation project.

3. *Solicitation and development—hardware vendor selection.* At this point, Alpha Dental identified vendors for hardware, wrote Requests for Proposals, and followed up with bid analysis. For

example, they created a list of candidate vendors for each category by combining their current vendor list with other vendors gathered from trade magazines. With the list compiled, they wrote RFPs containing both a cover letter describing the project intentions and specifications that the vendors could use to create their price and performance proposals. When Alpha Dental received the completed proposals, they ranked them based on factors such as price and quality and created a "short list" of the best qualified vendors in order to interview the top three candidates.

4. *Software vendor selection.* Alpha Dental identified vendors of off-the-shelf software, wrote Requests for Proposals, and performed bid analysis. The software vendor selection process was very similar to the hardware vendor process described previously. However, software vendors were willing to provide evaluation copies for free (or a nominal charge such as $15) in order to test the characteristics of the software. These software evaluation programs (working models of the actual products) and demonstration programs (programs loaded with sample data and tutorial manuals) enabled the review team to perform better product selection.

5. *Documentation development.* Early in the project, it was suggested that they create custom Alpha Dental documentation to supplement the User Manuals provided by the suppliers of software and hardware. The outcome was a document that acted as an introduction to the hardware and software tools available to the sales and marketing representatives and their managers. Further, they developed training material, reference guides, and a help-desk system.

6. *Supplemental services.* In an installation as large as Alpha Dental, some unique software customizing was needed. These were nonprogramming changes—changes that could be made easily using the user-definable aspects of the software. Alpha Dental rejected any ideas of having a custom system designed for their company. The costs were too high (estimates started at $600,000), and the lead time was too long (more than a year). Nonprogramming customizing consisted of sales script

designation, user-definable field creation, prospecting and account management letter creation and password protection, and privilege levels development. These changes enabled Alpha Dental to customize the software to their specific company's needs without expensive programming.

7. *Procurement.* Procurement is the process of acquiring all the components and services. Details regarding shipping requirements, remittance conditions, and legal aspects of quality and performance guarantees were specified. The contracts administrator at Alpha Dental was instrumental in bringing this aspect of the project to a successful completion.

The following is a generalized list of what was procured for this project. Alpha Dental considered the following equipment: laptop/notebook computers with cases and modems, communication equipment (modems), printers, local area networks (LANs), desktop PCs, cables, off-the-shelf software, Sales Ally account management software, communications software to send and receive account information from the field to the home office, spreadsheet software for data analysis, mapping software to map account information and territories on a region-by-region basis, and installation and testing services.

Other activities conducted in this phase included serializing the hardware and software components (creating a list of a components to be dispersed and assigning them a serial number to track them for repair and inventory), preparing equipment to be delivered to the field sales reps, assigning user IDs and password formats and strategies, creating an accounting system for users on the system, and establishing data security and backup protection procedures. User involvement increased slowly as each hardware or software element was introduced.

8. *The installation and testing phase.* The purpose of the installation and testing phase was to allow dedicated time for bringing together hardware components and software elements. At Alpha Dental, a prototype system was installed and *alpha* and *beta* tested (these are computer code words for the first and second test runs) prior to introducing it to the pilot sales force

participants. Alpha testing consisted of software and hardware testing by the system installer on a few units to confirm operation, and beta testing consisted of testing all the system components in the hands of a few selected field sales representatives, regional managers, and home office managers.

9. *Laptop/notebook PC and local area network preparation.* Prior to use, Alpha Dental verified equipment operation, installed operating systems and network software, conducted site preparation and cabling, conducted hardware and software installation and configuration, and installed pretyped databases and report formats, a menu program, and help screens.

10. *Testing.* Following installation, Alpha Dental tested the communication links, networks, and application software. The communication links offered the greatest challenge due to the complexity of the hardware, software, and data transmission paths. Each of these links was first tested by the installer, secondly by a few select sales representatives, and finally by the pilot team members. A dry run of the communication process was conducted for a full month prior to complete involvement by all the project participants.

11. *Implementation.* Following the installation and testing of all hardware and software components, the actual implementation of the pilot began. The pilot team consisted of selected members of the future user group. At this point, Alpha Dental sales representatives, managers, and other users began taking an active role as the pilot proceeded. At first, they used sample data files that were designed to test various characteristics of the database and data transfer process, but they began using live data as soon as they confirmed database integrity and data communication accuracy.

    It was necessary to assign a clerical employee to type records into Sales Ally to populate the database, thus allowing the account representatives uninterrupted selling time. The team conducted training preparation sessions to train the trainers, and they prepared support services for the ultimate needs of the end-users.

12. *Training.* Training occurred during several phases including installation and testing, implementation, and the formal Alpha Dental training program. For example, the LAN manager and sales managers were trained prior to the implementation phase. The training services included the following: a training facility that would be used to house samples of each of the components, instructional lecture materials and demonstration hardware and software; a computer introduction on PCs set up with the actual application software; application training by way of classroom lecture and automated learning demonstrations provided by the software and hardware manufacturers; an introduction to connectivity elements; evaluation forms used to analyze sales improvement due to system implementation; and enhancement of computer-based training programs for individual learning opportunities. Each of these training services familiarized users with different aspects of the system and ensured a consistent approach to the teaching process.

13. *Support.* In order to maximize project benefits at Alpha Dental, support was provided to sales representatives, sales managers, and marketing planning personnel. Elements of the support services included day and evening telephone hot-lines, dial-up and on-site support, software updates, support call logging, and follow-up. An 800 number telephone line enabled field users to call company headquarters and talk to a trained assistant who could help with field problems or confusion. Further, a separate facsimile (fax) number was set up for users to question the help-desk by fax. Reply was possible either by a follow-up telephone call or fax message. A representative of the Information Systems Group planned a quarterly field visit to provide closer service to field users. Each telephone call, communication, or action of a field user was recorded to provide continuity in assistance and to provide the basis for future analysis of the help-desk activity. Alpha Dental tracked all these actions with Sales Ally. The names, titles, addresses, and voice and fax telephone numbers of all the employees were entered into a master help-desk database. Notes of each

conversation, including difficulties encountered when using the system, were recorded for each user. The help-desk used Sales Ally functions to support the field users, their managers, and the system support personnel.

14. *Project evaluation.* In order to assess the efficacy of the pilot project, an evaluation was conducted using interviews and questionnaires. One action was the development and analysis of evaluation forms that contained questions such as "How much time did it take you to learn the system in order to be comfortable using it on a daily basis?" and "What are the features of the system which give you the greatest benefit?" These evaluation forms provided the foundation for an annual project review compendium. Another action was a compilation of support calls and statistics for analysis of the most common errors, failures and misjudgments. In addition, a management report and a statistics document were created to highlight the system benefits to management. Finally, a "new requirements definition" document was created to define additional features and functions to be added to the current system . . . a "wish list" for future expansion.

15. *Application software and hardware updates.* In order to keep the system current, Alpha Dental made provision for keeping abreast of both software and hardware improvements. They considered the following: additional follow-up training and support, documentation updates, and Alpha Dental turnover training. Software updates were provided by the software vendors, all with differing update policies. For example, the Sales Ally update policy consists of a $100 fee for each new release issued.

To stay abreast of hardware improvements or changes, Alpha Dental registered their equipment with the manufacturers by returning the completed registration cards provided with the products. Further, they encouraged the manufacturers' sales representatives to visit the Alpha Dental home office on a quarterly basis in order to keep abreast of new technology.

What Was Purchased

As a result of the research conducted, Alpha Dental purchased and implemented an automated sales and marketing support system consisting of the following components and services.

The Hardware

Local area networks and workstations:

- 6 Intel-based 386 file servers (1 for each region)
- 250 notebook PCs to act as stand-alone units or to act as workstations connected to the file server
- Cables and connections for each CPU
- 6 laser printers, 1 for each file server for printing letters or maps or creating reports
- 280 modems (with the extra stored in event of failure) to be used to send and receive information
- 6 fax/modems to be used with file servers to support the fax mail feature of Sales Ally
- 6 color monitors for file servers
- 200 specialized brief cases/carrying cases for the field sales representatives' notebook computers

The Software

- DOS operating system and Novell networking software
- 260 single-user Sales Ally integrated application software packages
- 7 network versions of Sales Ally
- 7 Borland Quattro spreadsheet software packages
- Ally Data Link, file communication and transfer software from Scherrer Resources, Inc.—a software tool to send and receive data from the field to the 6 regional offices and from the 6 regions to the home office. Packages were purchased for 300 remote nodes and 7 hosts.

- 7 *Mapping Software* packages (MapInfo Corporation)—displays account locations, 1 for each file server, and 1 for the home office

Training Services Conducted

Alpha Dental created a training group specifically dedicated to this project. First, the training group trainers were trained. They, in turn, trained the end users in all aspects of the system. Training occurred in each of the six regional office locations as part of a quarterly sales meeting. Training took a total of eight hours—four hours on each of two days of the quarterly sales meeting.

Support Services Created

The Information Services Group at Alpha Dental provided all support services to users of the sales and marketing system. A telephone hot line was designated and was staffed from 8 a.m. to 10 p.m. Eastern Time to allow for a nationwide time coverage for the regional representatives. In addition, each of the regional offices had a designated support person who helped to troubleshoot any problems that might occur. The employment descriptions of all people involved were modified to show that each was responsible for some aspect of the automated system. Each person was given a salary raise commensurate with a recognition that the maintenance and support of the computer system was a valuable and strategically important activity.

Immediate Project Benefits

Our Stealth system sales representative, Tom Smith, jumped into the new system quickly. He was able to transfer all his old prospect files into the new system through an ASCII file format file conversion process. He even helped the others who used the Stealth system to convert to the new integrated package. Within months, Tom was on top of his sales goals and exceeded his quota. Two out of three of the quarterly sales award winners were users of the new integrated system and made speeches in sales meetings about the virtues of this system.

Realized Goals of the Integrated Sales Support System

The earlier enumerated goals of the Integrated Sales Support System were reviewed by the project team after one year of operation. These were their findings:

- *Increased sales representative productivity.* Through the use of this automated sales support system, each of the sales representatives experienced an improvement in at least one aspect of his or her business, whether it was appointment managing, call reporting, or prospect tracking. The average number of accounts that could be managed efficiently by a single representative grew from 120 to 160, a 33 percent increase. Calls increased from 50 to 100 per month, a 100 percent gain. Numbers of account follow-up letters increased by 30 percent as a result of the ease of creating and sending letters using the software.
- *Increased customer satisfaction.* Many of Alpha Dental's customers commented on the increased level of attention they were receiving from their sales representatives. Client retention was increased as customer satisfaction grew. Clients sent numerous letters stating that their representatives were "the best," and sales representative morale increased overall.
- *Increased reporting speed and capability.* The Information Systems Group was able to create more comprehensive and up-to-date reports as a result of using their Sales Ally software program. Daily data consolidation gave the president and all senior officers current information on account managing and prospecting activities. The company-wide availability of this account information made it possible for sales representatives to get help closing business that may have eluded them otherwise. Win/loss analysis was conducted more quickly, which helped product managers make changes to product features for buyer adoption. This, in turn, made it possible for production managers to increase production earlier on improved products and to reduce production on expired or unfavorable products before they ended up in undeliverable stockpiles.

- *Increased company profitability.* Company profitability increased over the long term because each sales representative could effectively handle more accounts, enabling Alpha Dental to expand its coverage and market share using the same number of sales representatives. Further, as a result of bringing information more rapidly to the home office from field sales representatives, the sales cycle was reduced from an average of five to four weeks. This resulted in an immediate annual revenue increase of 20 percent.

- *Controlling versus reporting—looking forward.* Sales managers were able to initiate a new sales promotion within days rather than months. This quick response mechanism gave Alpha Dental the ability to launch strategic sales initiatives more quickly and to measure the response with greater specificity.

  For example, when Alpha Dental launched a new product, they had already received competitive pricing information from field sales representatives only weeks earlier. Thus, when they launched their new product, it was priced aggressively and competitively. As they used Sales Ally to target-mail the announcement, the sales reps could see which accounts got the announcement and which had not. This helped everyone plan their time and material resources accordingly. Further, the sales support system enabled managers to query the account base to determine the material and production requirements needed to accommodate future orders of new products brought to market. The database could be cross-queried for the likelihood of ordering certain types of dental supplies based on the clients' past orders and new product feature sets. This helped Alpha Dental minimize waste in purchasing raw inventory for product production.

- *Reduced cost of operation.* With fewer competing information systems, Alpha Dental now can focus its resources more efficiently and effectively. Redundancy in system function has been eliminated. Data is entered only once into the central system, thus saving data-entry time. As a result, computers have begun supporting the company and its sales force, rather than people supporting the operation of computers.

Further, the plan to expand the sales operation to other countries is underway because the costs of expansion are now less.

Sailing Success

Other nonquantifiable successes in the installation of the sales and marketing automation system at Alpha Dental include the following. Sally Jones, programmer/analyst with newly found freedom, entered and won the horticultural award for the most beautiful succulents in her county home-garden exhibition. Tom Smith, sales representative and super salesman with weekends now free, took up golfing and became so good he was asked to join the club on its national tour. Jan Clatchy was retrained and now creates beautiful forms and documents using the Sales Ally custom report generator and teaches computing classes at night to local PC user-groups. Ben Bradley, western regional sales manager and known for bringing home the bacon, realized a lifelong dream and became a gourmet chef at a downtown restaurant on weekends. The Alpha Dental president, Dick Cranston, made the cover of *Sailing News* with the caption "'Selling Sailor,' How Alpha Dental Computerized Its Sales Force and Now Sails Along." The cover picture showed Mr. Cranston with a notebook computer on the deck of his fully outfitted sailing and selling boat/office. Now, with their accounts under control and their clients happy, the Alpha Dental employees have more time for happiness and good living. (Don't laugh—this could happen to your company!)

■ ■ ■

Follow-along Demonstration with Included Software

Included with this book is a fully functioning copy of the Sales Ally software program. Sales Ally is a nationally recognized sales support software product in use in both large and small companies and is the software selected by Alpha Dental. By installing this software onto your computer, you can follow along and see how Tom Smith, sales representative at Alpha Dental, became Sales Representative of the Year. On your own, you can try a sample installation of this integrated sales and marketing software program and follow step-by-step the actions taken to get the system up and running.

The Sales Ally software is provided to readers who may want to implement sales support software at their own company or for themselves as sales representatives. Should you wish to start up a sales and marketing automation project at your company, you may use the enclosed software as a benchmark against which to compare other products.

Installation

Software installation is as easy as inserting the first diskette into drive A of the computer and typing *Install* at the A prompt. From then on, simply read the on-screen instructions.

`Insert first diskette into Drive A`

`Obtain C:> prompt`

Type **A:** <Enter>

At A:> prompt type **Install** to put program on hard disk <Enter>

To run program type **SA** <Enter>

Getting Oriented

Sales Ally is an integration of an account record database and a word processing letter generator. Further, it contains specialized features such as an activities calendar and software maintenance and set-up functions. Each of these main functions can be viewed on the main menu of Sales Ally (see Figure 14.1). After typing *SA* (an abbreviation for Sales Ally*)*, you can view these functions.

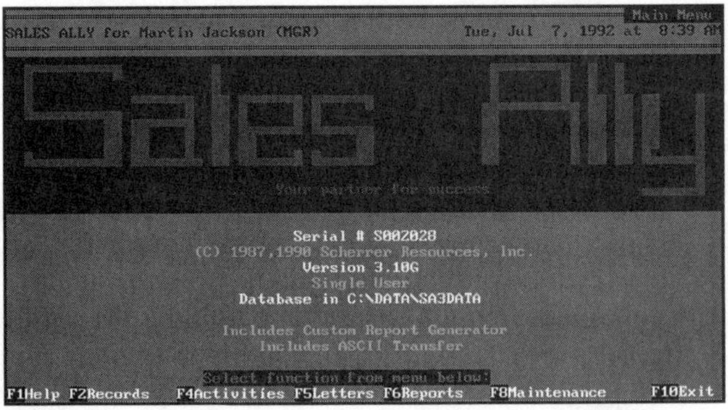

Figure 14.1 View of Main Menu screen in Sales Ally

Help is always available by pressing the F1 key. Tom used this system to learn about new features and to refresh his memory on other things he had learned in training. The function F10 Quit is used to escape from screens and to leave the program. All data is saved as you exit the program. Tom was able to identify where he was in the program by viewing the menu path shown at the top right of the screen. The functions at the bottom of the screen led him to the new areas of the program.

Entering Records and Accounts

You can enter your own account records from your current manual database and experiment with features and functions of Sales Ally. Selecting F2 Records and Add allows you to add either contact records or company account records (see Figure 14.2). Although the Information Systems Group at Alpha Dental automatically entered most of Tom's accounts, Tom manually entered newer accounts not yet in the system. He purchased a list of leads on floppy disk from a specialized mailing list company and loaded the leads using the ASCII upload feature found in F8 Maintenance.

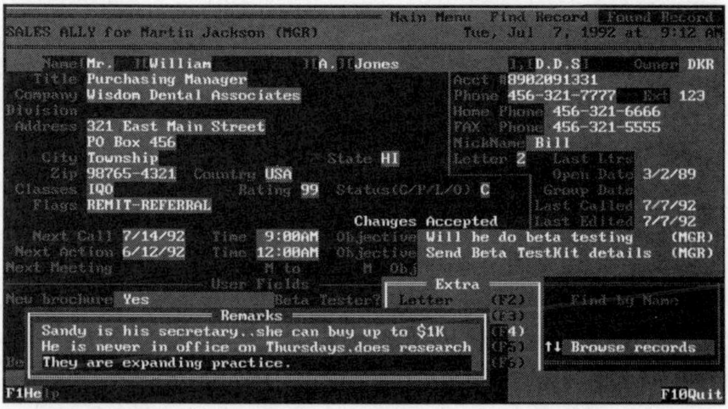

Figure 14.2 Customer and Prospect Record screen of Sales Ally

Tom entered the name, title, company name, address, and account numbers of all his accounts. Further, he established classes of accounts based on his customer profiles—end buyers, resellers, hospitals, dental offices, health care centers, and other classes of customers. He also rated them numerically (one through ten from least likely to buy to most likely to buy) using the rating field. The status field allowed him to define whether the contact person was a lead (status L), a prospective client (status P), or a client/customer (status C). This helped him to establish the benchmarks for measuring the sales cycle duration. He even entered the names of his friends and acquaintances as other (status O).

`Press F2 Records`

`Press Add Record`

`Type` **`Mr.`** `for salutation <Enter>`

`Type` **`First Name`** `<Enter>`

`Type` **`Middle Initial`** `<Enter> and` **`Last Name`** `<Enter>`

`Continue until all fields are entered with information`

Entering Notes

During each conversation, Tom was able to record notes using the notepad in Sales Ally. Each note is automatically date- and time-stamped. If a manager writes something in his or her notepad, he or she can reread it and react to it on a daily basis. Quick letters can also be stored in the notepad so that they can be reviewed.

`While on Record Screen:`

`Select F7 Notes (observe the date and time stamp on the screen)`

`Type in the words of the conversation`

`Zoom up Notepad with F3 Zoom if you wish full screen view`

`Select F10, Quit, and the notes will be automatically saved`

Entering Appointments and Schedules

You can enter appropriate activities such as call appointments, actions, and meeting dates. You can schedule them for specific dates and times. You can also document the objectives of the calls and actions and define the lengths of the meetings. Tom used this area first to schedule a phone call to schedule a meeting. When the meeting was completed, he scheduled future actions including follow-up calls. This process enabled him to keep on top of his accounts and be more responsive to his customers.

`While in a Record select F5 Schedule`

`Notice the Schedule Box Window in the center of the screen`

`To set a call for seven days from now, type` **`7`** `<Enter>`

`To set the time for 2pm, type` **`2`** `<Enter>`

`Type in the words for` **`Objective of Call, Follow-up`** `<Enter>`

`At this point, you can select F10 to Quit Schedule or select Set Action Date & Time, or Meeting Date & Time`

`Use same steps as above for setting Actions and Meetings`

`(You can type actual dates or number of days from now)`

Reviewing and Conducting Today's Activities

Under F4 Activities, you can review a list of all calls, actions, or meetings scheduled for today. They are configured in three vertical columns. Tom used these to keep up with his accounts. Each day before he left the office for a field sales call, he would bring up this screen and review his day. In some cases, he would print out a copy to take with him or take a notebook computer along with him.

`From Main Menu select F4 Activities`

`Notice the three vertical columns`

`With right, left, up, and down arrow keys, highlight name`

`Press <Enter> to select the person to view`

`<DP>Now you are ready to call, take notes, or write letters`

Activities are either calls, actions, or meetings. Calls are actual personal sales calls or telephone calls. Sales Ally depicts the total scheduled for that day on the top of the screen. To the right is a list and tally of the actions scheduled for that day. For example, Tom scheduled his proposal writing and delivery tasks in the actions area. To the right of this is the meetings column. Tom entered the start and end time for all meetings, and Sales Ally tracked the meetings and displayed them in the meetings column of the Activities screen (see Figure 14.3).

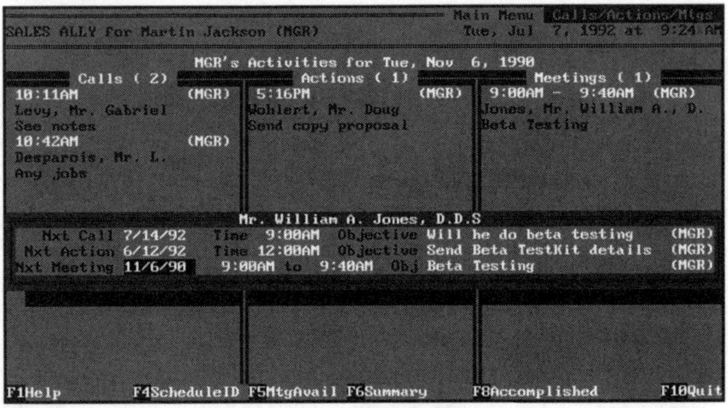

Figure 14.3 Activities screen showing scheduled calls, actions, or meetings

Entering Account Histories

With each record profile is a file of information describing the historical contacts made or actions taken on this account. The historical information is automatically collected by the program as the sales representative makes a call or takes an action. These histories are found with each record.

As Tom accomplished a call, action, or meeting, Sales Ally automatically entered a one-line entry into the history file stating the scheduled and the actual dates of the action and the objective accomplished. These one-line entries are valuable review items used by managers to monitor the disposition of accounts.

Entering Letters

You can enter your own prospect and sales letters and even do a mailmerge with your newly created database. You can enter letters for client follow-up or for new account prospecting.

Tom had the benefit of having the company pre-enter letters into his letter directory. They gave him 10 letters on topics such as the following: "Thank You for the Order," "Why Haven't We Heard from You?" and "I'm Sorry about the Mix-Up." These were powerful account management letters that were used nationwide at Alpha Dental. In some circumstances, Tom used his own letters to deliver the right message (see Figure 14.4).

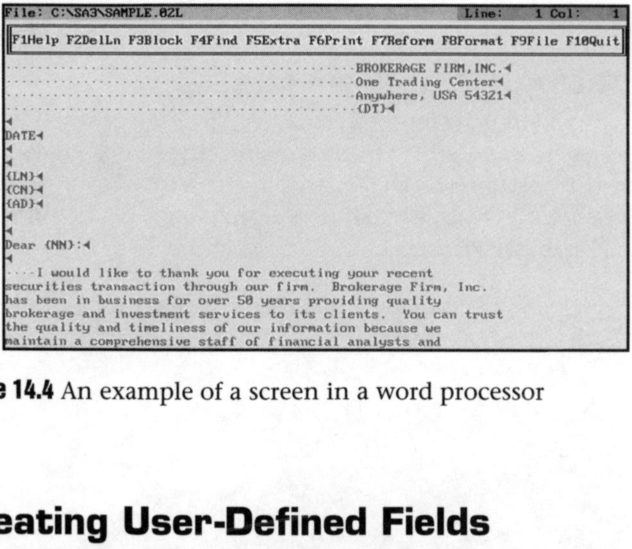

Figure 14.4 An example of a screen in a word processor

Creating User-Defined Fields

User-defined fields are found at the bottom of both the contact records and the company records. These fields have no headings until the user enters them into the appropriate area in Software Maintenance. For example, a field could have the name Annual Revenue, Number of Employees, or Order Frequency.

Tom helped Alpha Dental configure the software for his specific needs. He defined some of the fields as Secretary's Name, Birthdate, and Favorite Activities in order to support his desire to give personalized attention to his customers (see Figure 14.5).

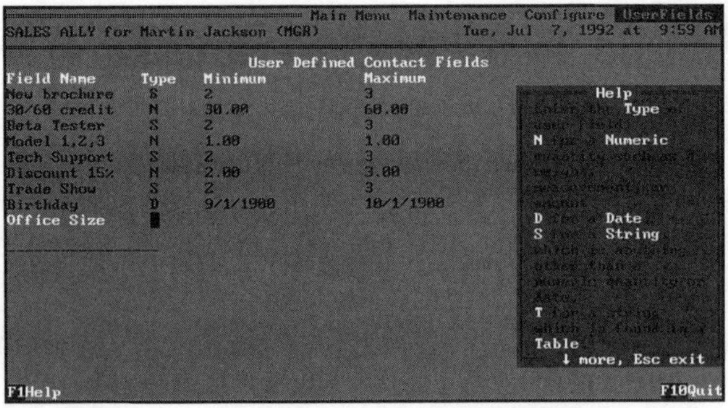

Figure 14.5 Set-up screen for user-definable fields for Record screen

Creating Sales Forecasts

Sales Ally enables the user to enter forecasted orders into the order-entry system. By entering an order and putting a future sales date on it, the order becomes an element in a forecast sales report. Tom also used the forecast feature to define the probability of closing the sale on that date (see Figure 14.6).

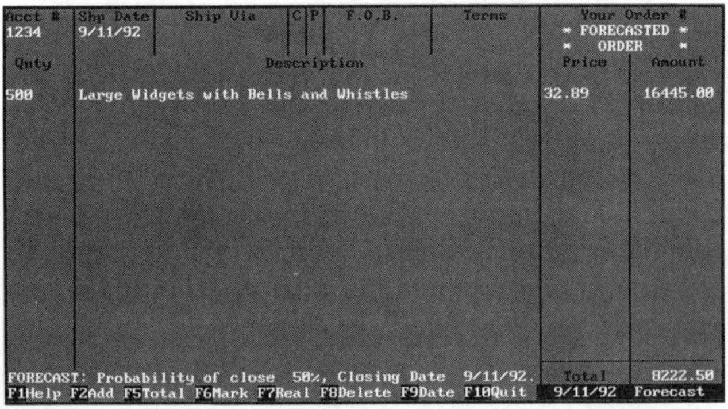

Figure 14.6 Sales forecasts defined as future orders with percentage probability of closing

Entering Expense Accounts

Tom uses the Module for Time and Expense Reporting as a method of recording his business-related expenses. He types the expenses into the computer and allocates them to accounts. The aggregate report is segregated and organized so that he receives his expense reimbursement checks more quickly. The enclosed software includes an expense account journal for entering expenses incurred in your own business. You can enter expenses and track them by account number or job code. You can enter auto, hotel, food, and miscellaneous expenses into this journal.

Printing Reports

Sales Ally comes complete with dozens of preformatted report forms. You can print all records in account number order, by call, or by appointment date.

```
From Main Menu select F6 Reports

Highlight the report needed (e.g., Name Address Listing)

Select Standard Format

Select F6 to Display or F7 to Print

Include only Contact Records

Define which records are for output by filling in blanks

Select PgDn (Page Down) key to move to next screen

Select PgDn again to begin sorting process
```

Creating Your Own Customized Report Formats

The Information Systems Group at Alpha Dental designed special custom reports for use by managers and sales representatives. These specialized reports were used to report active accounts in trouble, high-volume accounts, and accounts being transferred to new sales representatives. Tom also created some of his own report formats to give him a better picture of his territory resulting in increased sales.

The report he created was a "last edited" report that showed him the people with whom he had made contact during the quarter. When he compared this with his account listing report, he was able to pinpoint, on a quarterly basis, the weak accounts in his territory that needed more attention.

You can try your hand at creating custom reports by selecting Custom Reports in the Report section of Sales Ally.

Entering Sales Scripts

Sales Scripts are collections of words and phrases that can be used in a selling circumstance to help you remember key ideas. Alpha Dental used this area of Sales Ally to create competitive information in reference to the products of other vendors. This information enabled all sales representatives to compete more effectively and to close business more frequently.

```
At C:> outside of program type scredit <Enter>

Select script you wish to edit <Enter>

Enter phrases you wish to add or modify

Save them with the Save command

Leave the script edit function with Quit

Return to Sales Ally by typing SA <Enter>

View scripts by pressing Alt and Shift at the same time
```

Running Other Programs

Sales Ally has an auxiliary program feature that lets you bring to the screen other programs on your hard disk while you are in Sales Ally. By combining the Control and F4 keys, you can activate other software programs. The same function is also available under Control F5 and Control F6. These functions are often known as windowing or toggling functions that bring you from one software application program to another without entering a DOS-level command or abandoning Sales Ally.

Alpha Dental used the auxiliary program function to bring up spreadsheet and electronic mail programs. This action required fewer keystrokes and less difficulty than exiting the program and returning to DOS to run the next software application. Speed was increased and more could be accomplished in less time.

Dig In!

With this brief example, you can see why Tom Smith became one of the top sales people in his company. Not only did he have his own good ideas, but he executed them effectively with the support of a powerful portable computer hardware and software system. To experience the power of your own computer, feel free to install the included software and use it. It has all the functions that Tom Smith used to become a successful sales representative.

■ ■ ■

Case Study 2

Integrated Financial Client Support System

In the following case study, a registered investment advisor uses an integrated software system for selling financial securities. The case study describes the functions of the software, the selection of a portable computer, and the application for account management. It focuses on the software's specific features that bring benefits to both the investment advisor and his clients.

The Background

Team Advisors, Inc., a financial subsidiary of Excelsior Bank & Co., was founded in 1934 and is based in New York City. Currently, this bank maintains more than 500 registered brokers and investment advisors in more than 85 bank branch offices throughout the United States. Team Advisors' registered securities brokers and advisors represent financial products, such as stocks, bonds, limited partnerships, government funds, mortgage insurance, life insurance, and commercial paper. Team Advisors is recognized as one of the largest retail securities organizations within a banking environment in the country.

Professional Development

The training of new brokers is highly emphasized at Team Advisors. Recognizing that one of its greatest assets is the professional quality of its staff, the bank invests a great deal of time and effort in assisting its retail brokers and investment advisors in becoming better financial product sales representatives. Each new representative spends several weeks in corporate-level training before being assigned to a branch office. Once assigned, the reps are assisted by office managers and other support services so that they are able to give their clients the best investment service possible.

The Problem—Service Is the Key to Success

As the banking and financial services environment has changed, so have the process and procedure of selling financial services. Since banking organization changes (brought about by modifications to the Glass-Steagall Act of 1933), banks have begun to compete with traditional retail channels in the sales of financial products and services. Each channel has its advantages, but both need to focus on the "service advantage" now more than ever.

The service advantage can be loosely described as that collection of actions or products which increase the level of customer satisfaction. The measurement of this level of customer satisfaction is often the amount of repeat business retained by the selling organization. Examples of repeat business include the following: insurance renewals, new products purchased, and cross-selling of one product with another.

This case study describes one way that Team Advisors, Inc., increased its level of service to its customers. The personal computer managers at Team Advisors helped their brokers and financial advisors by offering guidance in the selection of business-enhancing tools. These tools included computers, fax machines, software, and other sales aids.

How To Get Better Service

Client service can be measured in terms of satisfaction observed by repeat business. After interviewing hundreds of customers who ceased doing business with Excelsior Bank, Team Advisors noted that two barriers came up more frequently than others. The first was the concept of how the customers felt about the institution. Statements like "It is impersonal," "I feel cold," or "I am only a number," characterized the moods of departing customers. The second barrier seemed to be the match of products with the needs of the customer. "There did not seem to be any need to connect with this bank," was one response often heard, despite the fact that Excelsior was considered a full-service financial establishment having 80 percent of all financial product offerings under one roof! Clearly, something was missing. The magnifying glass became focused on personalized service.

The Front Line

The front line of any organization is the sales force, and as such, its power to build or destroy an organization is ever present. It became very clear that the frontline sales force needed to provide better service. But what? They already had the best sales training, the best-looking offices, the fastest-typing secretaries, and the brightest college graduates and professional advisors. The sales material was beautiful; the product was priced competitively; and the post sales support was the best in the industry. What more could they do?

When they posed the question, "What more can we do?" someone responded, "That is the answer! The question is not 'What more can we do?' but 'How can we do more?' Let's just do more of the good stuff we are doing now!" That became the guideline for the strategic plan that evolved from a small boardroom meeting in an aging bank building in New York City.

The Solution—Power Tools!

The sales managers at Excelsior's Team Advisors Group decided they wanted to do two things better: handle more people without sacrificing service quality and provide more customized product offerings. They decided the first could be handled by better account management and more frequent calls and the second with a database management software system.

The team described the needed functions and came up with two separate descriptions. A telemarketing team was needed for the first objective of more frequent customer/client contact, and a marketing software program was needed to query the database for efficient cross-sell opportunities.

By surprise, the sales support team found their solution in a single software program that advertised the following features: integrated database management and word processing, database sorting, financial product tracking, autodialing, note-taking, call scheduling, and report creation. It was billed as a financial product sales support software program for personal computers, and its price was only $395. A single network version for a whole office was only $1,895. It seemed inexpensive and powerful. But was it adaptable to their needs, especially to the needs of the sales representatives who wanted to be in the field more frequently with their portable computers?

The Testing Process

After reviewing Broker's Ally software, from Scherrer Resources, Inc., Team Advisors made this software available to a pilot group of five of its best sales representatives. If this software could perform the functions advertised, could adapt easily to their banking needs, and could fire up the velocity of customer contact, then it could be used in all of the branches.

More on Broker's Ally

Broker's Ally is the most widely used software package among retail securities brokers. Ron Farmer, Vice President, Investments, has been a successful broker at this bank for six years. He was one of the five pilot sales representatives using Broker's Ally. He began by installing it on a desktop computer and having his accounts typed in by the sales assistant. He then began using it to manage his sales activities and to keep track of clients, prospects, and their investment objectives.

Ron took great care to ensure that as he classified customers, he really knew their investment goals and objectives. After he had cataloged his database as such, he was sure he could cross-sell appropriate products to his customer base. "Cross-selling with a crossbow," he thought.

Cross-Selling Example

Ron had been selling municipal bonds for years and maintained a list of 435 customers who had purchased various types of bonds. Because these investors were usually interested in the tax advantage characteristics of municipal bonds, Ron recognized that they might be interested in one of the new offerings his company had for sale.

Ron performed a letter mailmerge function in Broker's Ally and printed 435 "New Offering" letters presenting the product prospectus to potential investors. Immediately after printing the letters, he set up call-back dates of three days from then for those candidate investors. After three days, he called the names that came up in his calls list. To his delight, he found that three out of five people purchased this new product, thus selling out the offering within three days of his cross-selling campaign.

All the Information Now in His Computer

At first, Ron worried that having all of his customer information in his computer would leave him vulnerable to loss of information. But, after months of backing up his data onto diskettes, he became comfortable with this procedure. Further, using the custom report generator in Broker's Ally, Ron printed special lists of client names and account numbers as added backup.

Ron found that incorporating Broker's Ally into his marketing plan gave him the support he needed to increase the number of contacts he could make. It was a great relief when he left the office one day with no lead cards, account folders, or message pads left on his desk.

The computer had changed his way of doing business. "With Broker's Ally, nothing slips through the cracks. It forces you to keep up," said Ron.

Does More in Less Time

Ron Farmer now has many more people to track, yet he tracks them better than before. He has effectively doubled his throughput. At first, he thought he needed a computer system just to keep up, but now it gives him the power to push ahead.

With the help of the sales management group, he was the first to be selected for the use of a portable notebook computer. This portable enabled him to take his account information with him into the field while making personal sales calls. He uses Broker's Ally to take notes, send letters, make calling lists, and mail company newsletters to his 1,300 clients and prospects. Also, by using the auxiliary program feature of Broker's Ally, Ron can move easily around his hard disk. He can quickly switch from one program to another at a keystroke.

After five years at Team Advisors, Ron has discovered that Broker's Ally allows him to do more work in less time and helps him keep his business growing. "I use Broker's Ally religiously. It is on the screen first thing in the morning," said Ron.

Branch Automation

Through the purchase of a site license for Broker's Ally for $100,000, Excelsior Bank was able to computerize each of its 500 Team Advisors sales staff. Both desktop and notebook computers were purchased in bulk and are currently supported by the bank's Information Systems group. The dream of doing more in less time has become a reality. After all, wasn't that the dream of the computer revolution?

■ ■ ■

Case Study 3

A Computerized Real Estate Sales and Prospecting System

The following case study describes the actions of a single residential real estate agent using a notebook computer to improve his sales performance. It describes the information-gathering problems encountered by real estate professionals who want to use personal computers to perform routine sales and prospecting tasks. This sales agent is a member of a national real estate franchise network and works independently through a franchise office in Denver, Colorado.

This discussion highlights the sales agent's use of an integrated software package designed especially for real estate agents. Further, it describes the features of his integrated database software and the manner in which he integrates his portable computer into his sales activities. It describes the added efficiency and time savings resulting from the use of a portable computer.

Company Background

Bondwell Residential Realtors, Inc., is a nationally recognized residential real estate sales organization based in northern California. With approximately 350 offices and more than 3,800 agents, Bondwell ranks as one of the larger real estate establishments in the western United States. Founded in 1946, this franchise organization is enjoying rapid growth because it provides quality services and comprehensive support to its affiliated agents throughout the western United States.

Corporate Product Service Review and Approval

To increase profitability, Bondwell Realty personnel ensure that their agents receive the highest quality services available. One of the ways they accomplish this is by reviewing and selecting the products of various vendors for inclusion in their Approved Vendor program. Agents then know which vendors Bondwell Realty considers to be reliable and worthwhile. Given the growth of the use of personal computers and software, the corporate review team selects and approves a wide variety of appropriate PC software and hardware.

Franchise enterprises typically provide product review services to their members in order to help streamline business and improve performance for their members and themselves. The product review function is also used in corporations for employees but with less formality and structure. The product review function made the difference between wandering in the dark and a success story for the person in this case study.

One of the approved vendor tools selected by Bondwell Realty was Realty Ally software from Scherrer Resources, Inc. Realty Ally falls into a class of software called *agent productivity tools,* software that improves the speed and accuracy of activities conducted on a daily basis by real estate professionals. In its review, Bondwell Realty considered several aspects of the product: the software functions, the user manuals and documentation, the technical support, and the program's suitability for use by Bondwell Realty real estate agents.

Management contacted current users of the Realty Ally software, checked bank and vendor references, and concluded with a positive review. Scherrer Resources, Inc., and Realty Ally software became an approved software supplier to Bondwell Residential Realtors, Inc. The next process was to make the software *do something!*

Personal Background

Sam Telnill, a 10-year real-estate veteran, is a residential agent from the Bondwell Realty, Big Hill, Colorado, office. He is one of hundreds of Bondwell agents profiting from the franchise approved vendor review process. Having achieved Top Performer awards in four of his last six years, he was well on his way to independent income security. Sam discovered personal computers when a science teacher introduced him to the PDP-11 and the TRS-80. Although 12 years had passed since that time, he knew that someday he would utilize a personal computer to support his real estate profession. "Certainly," he thought, "if we can land a man on the moon, we should be able to make the routine process of matching real estate buyers with sellers more efficient."

The Problem—How To Make the Machine Do What You Want!

After the office manager purchased a personal computer for the secretaries to type letters, Sam bought an "inexpensive" database software program to enter his prospects. With the permission of the office manager, he installed the software onto this computer and read the manual to learn how to enter prospect names into the database. First, he had to set up the layout of the database. Was it to be keyed by name, by ZIP code, or by telephone number? Was it to be organized on the screen with the name or the listing number on top? Was it to be a relational database or a flat file?

During the process of reading the manual and setting up the software, the telephone rang. It was one of his contacts, and Sam was needed at the property immediately to correct inaccurate or incomplete paperwork or to fix an incorrect term in the contract. He was always having difficulty with the changing definitions and newly created mortgage offerings in the real estate business. He turned off the computer and jumped into his car to meet with his client. (In his need to move quickly, Sam forgot to save the changes he had made to his new database file and inadvertently lost his evening's work. He never discovered this problem because his evening of reading had convinced him that computers had not yet reached his level of need. He never looked at the $150 software again.)

The Solution—Specialized Real Estate Agent and Broker Software

Sam was introduced to the company's approved vendor selection process by the secretary who used the office personal computer. "Sam, perhaps you might find the software you need in this catalogue," she said. Sam spent the next evening reading the catalogue and perusing the trade journals for specialized real estate software. He listed a few candidates and decided to call one that sounded interesting. He compared it with his needs—database, appointment tracking, word processing, buyer/seller matching, autodialing, and label generating. He wanted to be sure that it would run on one of those "new fangled" portable computers that he had seen in the airport last week.

Sam set a budget and decided he would spend no more than $2,500 for the computer, the printer, and the software. He decided to choose the software first and get a recommendation from the software vendor as to which computer might be best for him and the software operation.

His vendor catalogue revealed a product that matched all of his specifications. He reviewed and purchased Realty Ally, from Scherrer Resources, Inc., through the corporate approved vendor catalogue. The cost was $395.

In discussing his hardware needs with the software vendor, the sales representative suggested a Zeos 386+ notebook computer with a special price offer of $1,795 (Zeos International, Ltd., 800-423-5891). It was rugged enough to sit on the front seat of his Bronco and take the abuse of his Rocky Mountain rides. It had the memory and storage necessary for the records he would keep—the 20 megabyte hard disk would hold 20 thousand prospects, properties, and people! Plenty of room for business expansion, he thought.

To round out the workstation, he bought an Okidata letter-quality printer for $400. The printer sales representative complimented Sam on selecting the software first. He also told Sam it was a good move to create a specification of functions for a system to meet his needs, something that would give him high quality and long-term service. Feeling good about his research efforts, Sam headed for home with his merchandise. He set up the system easily in his home office in about two hours. The disk operating system (DOS) was pre-loaded onto the computer. Installing the Realty Ally software took approximately five minutes, and plugging in the power cords and printer connection cord took 15 minutes more (mostly reading about parallel printer ports). He typed the command *RA* to run Realty Ally, and up it came on the screen display. He first added each component for a total bill using the built-in Realty Ally calculator, activated with two keys. $1,795 + $395 + $400 = $2,590. His previously set budget was on target, and he was in business!

Getting Started

One of the things Sam likes about his new system is its ease of use. Realty Ally has a self-running tutorial that he can run at any time to learn more about the functions of the software. Alt-1 is the key combination to activate the self-running slide show demonstration. It has taught him how to print labels, set up the printer, enter records and notes, and use the activity calendar scheduling functions.

Power Features for Ease of Use

Sam Telnill now uses Realty Ally each and every day of business. Realty Ally comes loaded with pretyped prospecting and special situation letters to speed the creation of correspondence. For prospecting, Sam modified the standard Realty Ally prospecting letter and saved it for his future use. He uses the pretyped "Welcome" letter and the envelope printing feature. He estimates that he saves 10 hours of work each month.

The Realty Ally on-line glossary of real estate terms enables Sam to review the definitions of certain real estate terminology. This guidance gives him the security of knowing that he is not likely to misdefine terms during the property settlement process, thus avoiding any last-minute delays.

Better Service

Sam uses the history report in Realty Ally to print a listing of all actions taken at a property on behalf of the seller. He itemizes the date and time of open viewing, the person(s) brought in, the conversations, and the objections to the sale. This detailed information makes it possible for him to keep more clients happier and to retain his listing longer. What once took him four hours per report now takes him 15 minutes for all client reports.

The Realty Ally calendar of actions can be printed on paper and carried to appointments in the event Sam chooses to leave his computer at home, although Sam rarely leaves his computer at home—it is a constant companion.

Sam uses Realty Ally to manage all of his real estate activities on a 386 notebook computer. He tracks all his clients, prospects, and potential listings in the Realty Ally database and uses the notepad to record conversations. He set up a category of records called Family and Friends and tracks their birthdays and special anniversaries.

Tracking Prospective and Expired Property Listings

One of the most powerful tasks that can be conducted by a computer is large database sorting and manipulation. Sam had always wanted to track a large number of households to advertise his ability to list and sell their property. With Realty Ally, he now conducts a systematic two-step prospecting campaign. Step one is the mailing of a service introduction letter. Step two is the follow-up of the letter with a telephone call. Realty Ally sets up this process automatically. As a result of conducting this automated two-step process, Sam has been able to increase his farming and prospecting area tenfold.

Both the Listing Expiration Date field and the Call-Back Date field help Sam prevent deals from falling through the cracks. He uses these features of Realty Ally to separate his prospective targets and to concentrate his energy where it is most lucrative.

Additional Speed Feature

Paperwork slows down all businesses, especially tax filing. Sam frequently uses the expense-account system built into Realty Ally to categorize and print reports of his business expenses, such as costs for open houses, advertising, travel, and hotels. Each of these costs can be categorized and printed to form an attachment to his IRS income tax deductions.

Sales Assistance Helps, Too

Sam and his sales associate, Kim Brone, who works in the local office, have decided they will never be without a computer. Together, they use it to track appointments, clients, and call-backs. Tracking "For Sale By Owners" is now a simple task for them, as is using the mailmerge feature to produce mass mailings to prospects in their area. Kim also uses the program to monitor all listed property in their geographic area in order to provide potential buyers with a wide selection of properties from which to choose.

"It goes on first thing in the morning and is turned off last thing at night. Though initially skeptical about the use of a computer, we could never be without our computer. It manages our whole business," said Kim.

Improved Efficiency and Client Satisfaction

With the use of his portable computer, printer, and Realty Ally software, Sam Telnill has improved his business and increased his sales level. The features that have helped him the most include the following:

- The portability of the computer (he was no longer desk bound)
- The integration of the database and word processor
- The ease of learning with the on-line tutorial

- The built-in power features, such as letters, report formats, and a glossary of real estate terms
- The fact that the software was especially designed for real estate professionals
- The on-line help keys
- His sales assistant's participation in the project
- The customer support line from the vendors of the computer, printer, and software.

The Time Has Arrived

Having seen it all come together, Sam now recognizes that the time for computers in real estate is today, not the future. With the creation of inexpensive portable computers and specialized real estate software, the power has come that he has been dreaming about since his science teacher first introduced him to comput rs in 1980. Now Sam is considered the office computing expert and is often found speaking at regional and national association meetings on the topic of agent productivity using computing technology. He is clearly on top of his profession.

■ ■ ■

Case Study 4

Using Portable Computers in Sales Presentations

This case study explores the ways in which a manufacturer's representative uses a portable computer to present sales presentations to clients. It explores the type of software and computer to use and the ways in which presentations can be made more effective. It describes the problems encountered when using this technology and how to work around them, and it elaborates on the success achieved.

Background

Larry Brill is a manufacturer's agent, also known as a manufacturer's representative. His job is to sell a broad line of electrical power and control products manufactured by various companies to a base of clients he has developed. These clients are located in his geographic territory of the states of Georgia and Florida and consist of electric utility companies, large and small municipalities, and commercial accounts. The products sold by Larry are distributed under an exclusive territory agreement, thereby preventing other vendors from offering the same products to his clients.

The Business Problem

In the sale of electrical power and control products, customers often like to view graphs, charts, and tables of equipment performance characteristics comparing one piece of equipment to another. Reps often carry briefcases full of specification sheets, product brochures, and warranty information.

With the advent of personal computers comes the ability to present complicated ideas based on the analysis of many data points in a single graph or chart. The power of the personal computer makes it possible to change these graphs or charts based on what-if scenarios and to show output immediately on the screen or from a printer.

The problem is how to use the personal computer in a sales environment to accomplish the goals of increased customer satisfaction and increased sales volume. The solution must come within a budget appropriate for a single sales representative. Larry Brill set a budget of approximately $4,000.

Background

Six months ago, Larry purchased a notebook computer advertised with a bright screen and loaded software onto it from the desktop computer located in his home office. He loaded inexpensive word processing and spreadsheet programs that he got at a low cost as throw-ins from the computer vendor. He explored the functions and features of these programs and took a stab at using them in his sales business.

How the Seed Was Planted

An interesting idea occurred to Larry as he carried his new notebook computer to a client business lunch. While sitting at the lunch table with the client, he removed his notebook computer from the case and put it on the table. He turned it on and logged into his client database software. Larry made a point to show his client the account records and took some time to review historic actions on the client's account. Larry reviewed past client orders, documented shipping destinations, and discussed future ordering plans as depicted on the screen in the client's record. Larry's idea was to show his client that he was a state-of-the-art representative dedicated to providing excellent service. The client was impressed; the lunch lasted a long time; and Larry got the order he sought.

Sparked by this experience, his customer asked, "Why don't you have all your product information in the computer . . . it sure would beat carrying around all those catalogs!" After reflecting on this, Larry carried the idea further. He believed that if he could use his notebook computer as a teaching aid, he might design software to illustrate components of the electrical equipment he represented. His notebook computer could act as a substitute slide projector and display cross sections of equipment, tools, and other electrical products.

Looking for Help

Having stumbled upon a method to increase sales through the use of a portable computer, Larry sought the guidance and support of his equipment manufacturers to produce some snappy screen illustrations. He pitched the idea of the manufacturers creating product demonstrations on floppy disks for personal computers.

Though the initial response by these manufacturers was positive, none came through with the type of software demonstration he wanted to see. He envisioned that they would create a state-of-the-art promotional display of the features and functions of their manufactured electrical control equipment. What he got were promises and referrals to other people within the company who might help him, but no follow-through. The people he contacted either seemed preoccupied with other computing initiatives, thought it might be someone else's domain, or simply did not care. Discouraged, he pursued the concept on his own.

What He Did

Using Presentation Express, an off-the-shelf software package from the Polaroid Corporation, Larry created a series of screens that allowed him to present the features of his product line to his customers. He hoped his customers would better understand the technical superiority of his products. This, in turn, would lead to improved sales.

Larry wanted his PC to give him a speed advantage over his competition. With his sales management software, he could quickly create customer profiles and quotes, print bills on the spot, and support his other client management activities. Now, with his presentation software, he was able to create sales presentations that would deliver powerful sales messages at a keystroke.

Larry's Research Process

Larry did some research to identify several products that could create an ideal PC system for sales presentations. He discovered that presentation (or illustration) software is a category of software that presents illustrations of ideas. Larry made a list of the broad categories of software and hardware he might use to help him create interesting presentations.

- Personal notebook computers to use for field presentations
- Monitors that look good for one-on-one sales presentations
- Software for creating presentations
- PC-based slide projection hardware for group displays
- Carrying cases to protect his equipment

After reading several magazines such as *PC Magazine, PC Computing, PC Week, Computer Shopper, Personal Selling Power,* and *Sales & Marketing Management,* he focused his search on the following ideas.

First, he gave up trying to find a slide projector system after recognizing that not only were the costs above his budget (usually greater than $3,000 for a complete system), but that most of his presentations were one-on-one or one-on-two, making a group presentation system unnecessary.

Secondly, he rejected the need for a carrying case because his sole piece of equipment would be his notebook computer, which already fit neatly into his accordion-expansion briefcase.

Thirdly, he found that his current screen (also called a monitor) was acceptable for his one-on-one style of presentations. Although he did not know it at the time, he had purchased a "backlit supertwist liquid crystal diode" (LCD) screen. These were fancy terms to him, but the computer experts considered it of acceptable quality and moderate price. Though it did not have the brightness of a gas plasma screen, it also did not have the extra $1,000 price tag. Besides, the gas plasma screens could not run on limited battery life. Armed with this information, he found he was satisfied with his original purchase. Now his focus shifted to software.

Larry narrowed his software search to three products: Freelance Graphics from Lotus Corporation, Aldus Persuasion from Aldus, and Presentation Express from Polaroid Corporation. He selected Presentation Express ($495) to help him with his project. Each of these products could perform similar functions, such as creating visual images for presentations and outputting to laser printers on plain paper or acetate overhead projector sheets or to photographic slide printers for slide projectors. Each could also be used to create on-screen visual displays. The following are the functions that Larry came to use.

- Display screens of text
- Display histograms and bar charts
- Display pie charts
- Use spacebar to move from screen to screen
- Use loop feature to repeat screen sequences
- Create automated screen shows
- Use time feature to pace the timing of automated display
- Use double buffering to improve screen response time

Larry created 20 screens that he uses in most sales calls. He created introductory screens about himself followed by screens that talk about the products he represents. He currently is doubling the number of screens he will use in his presentation to expand on specialty equipment features and benefits. The titles of the 20 are as follows:

1. Larry Brill, Manufacturer's Representative (his background)
2. Service Is the Key to My Success (his sales and service pitch)
3. Manufacturers I Represent (a list of manufacturers)
4. Products I Represent (a list of products by category)
5. Category Descriptions (a list of products further broken down)
6. Performance of Products (a graph showing performance)

7-17. Performance of Products (more performance screens)

18. Costs and Pricing (how he does his pricing)
19. My Service Orientation (a sales pitch on his service)
20. Conclusion (list explaining why customers should order from him).

Shown are examples of the display screens Larry created.

Larry Brill

Manufacturer's Representative

- Licensed professional engineer in Georgia and Florida
- Bachelor's and Master's degrees in electrical engineering
- 15 years experience in the selection, design, testing, and implementation of both large and small-scale electrical power and control equipment
- Former employers include Georgia Power & Light, General Electric, and Westinghouse
- Four years as manufacturer's representative

Figure 17.1 Screen 1 of his display sequence

Service Is the Key to My Success

In the Sales of Electrical Control and Power Products

- I handle a broad range of equipment categories
- I can obtain equipment from almost all manufacturers
- I offer excellent, competitive pricing
- I am knowledgeable
- I am experienced
- I am responsive
- I can do research for you
- I am your extra hand when you need it

Figure 17.2 Screen 2 of his display sequence

Time-of-Day Commercial Electric Meters

Top-of-the-Line Model

- Low service requirement
- Low cost
- Low long-term maintenance costs
- Utility-demand monitoring improvement
- Meets IEEE standards
- Low-profile design
- Newest design available

Figure 17.3 Screen 11, performance characteristics of time-of-day meters

Most of Larry's screens were text charts—title slides and bulleted lists. He used all of the four available text chart types: title, bullet, outline, and freeform text. He even created some charts in two-column format. Using Presentation Express, text will appear in the chart in the same order that you type it in on the screen, except for footnotes, which appear at the bottom.

Larry used the Screen Director function to create, preview, and proof graphic screens before he showed them. The Screen Director function was used to create on-screen presentations for situations that did not require slides or overheads. This function and others are found in most other presentation software packages. While displaying the screen, he used the spacebar to proceed to the next graphic. Later, he learned how to use the Loop Until Escape function to have the displayed screens repeat until he pushed the Escape (Esc) key. To pace his automatic display screen sequences, he set the Time Between Graphics feature at 10-second pauses between screens.

Because the creation of graphics is a computer memory-intensive process, the screen often appears to fade in as information is painted to the screen. Moving to each successive screen causes a fade lag time that can be disturbing to readers. Hence, Presentation Express offers a feature that enables the computer to create the screen in background mode and then quickly display it on demand. This is called *buffering*. It allows subsequent graphs to appear, fully drawn, on demand. Larry used this feature when he put his display in automated loop repeat mode.

Although his Presentation Express software enabled him to create fancy graphics such as shadowed text, stars, triangles, and checkmarks, he usually stuck with the basics and created simple, easy-to-read text screens.

Analysis of Setbacks

Although Larry's idea of having the manufacturers create PC sales presentations was a good one, it was not implemented because he did not know what software to suggest or to whom to present his idea. Larry failed to recognize that the manufacturers' job assignments came from elsewhere, usually the executive offices. Unfortunately, Larry was also branded a tinkerer and could not shake their perception that he wanted them to create expensive toys rather than usable sales presentations.

Larry was not talking to the right decision-makers. He may have gotten more support had he talked with the vice presidents of sales and marketing since sales productivity improvement is within their job descriptions. These two people may have been more motivated to push such an initiative, to obtain the right talent, and to fund the project.

How His System Accomplished His Goal

Larry's goal was to expedite his sales by creating a software sales presentation that conveyed valuable information to his clients. He hoped to increase his own income and that of the manufacturer through this process. Though he was unable to obtain presentation software from equipment manufacturers showing their products and features, he was able to create, on his own, a software sales presentation for use on his notebook computer.

Larry observed an interesting outcome as a result of using the system he had created. For certain types of products, his sales showed an increase, but for others, his sales remained constant. A review of the differences between these two categories quickly told him why. The products that sold more were products having multiple features, benefits, or ideas that benefitted from their enumeration and illustration. These were products that he considered difficult to sell but that offered him high commissions and offered the manufacturer high profit margins. The products that did not increase in sales volume as a result of illustration were commodity products that were considered to be universally understood and were staples of the industry.

Additionally, Larry found that his customers were responsive to his computer-based presentations and were impressed with his professional demeanor. They were curious about his computer and engaged him in extensive discussions, which usually fostered improved customer relations. Because he could quickly alter the screens as product features and benefits changed, he was perceived by his customers as always being on top of his product line.

Larry scaled back his idea of presenting equipment cutaways created by the manufacturer to showing more manageable screens such as features and benefits lists; thus, he was able to conduct the process on his own from start to finish. This gave him better control, more rapid response, and a customized, professional finish.

In conclusion, Larry found that the greatest return on his investment of time and money in illustration and presentation software and hardware was the detailing of more complicated and unique products. Happily, these were the same products that gave him the highest commissions and offered the manufacturing companies the highest profit margins.

■ ■ ■

18

Case Study 5

Database Marketing Project

The following case study explores the issues when the manufacturing company, Allegheny Steam Fittings, falls upon difficult times during a recession and learns to better utilize its current client base to improve sales performance. The case study will consider the effects brought on by recession, the negative morale brought on by these circumstances, the ideas discussed to bring about change, and the successful plan to cultivate improved client relations through database marketing techniques. It highlights the power of computer databases, portable computers, and data analysis. We will discuss the ideas that surfaced, the database functions that were keys to success, the role of the portable computer, and the costs and associated benefits.

The Background

Tom Harding is vice president of sales and marketing for Allegheny Steam Fittings, a multimillion-dollar manufacturing business. His revenue and resulting profits increased year after year in a decade-long march. Tom, the president, and the other members of the executive staff were amassing personal fortunes and living comfortably. They were positive, inspirational leaders in favorable times.

Then an economic decline eased its way into the business. Revenues sagged by 30 percent, profits dried up, and business hid in the closets. Customers went out of business, employees became grumpy, and sales representatives clamored for a bigger base salary. Would the impact of this recession be bankruptcy? Were the executive managers missing something? It was a time for soul-searching.

Interestingly, the answer to these problems resided within their reach. Most of the executive staff were not aware of the power of database marketing techniques and database analysis. Little by little, they fell into the answer. Here is the story of how database marketing, portable computers, and a rigorous sales plan helped pull them out of a personal recession and pave the way for a successful growth campaign.

Introspection

Tom Harding spearheaded a week-long retreat attended by Bill Somers, president; Ed Brown, VP manufacturing; and Holley Ruster, executive vice president. The focus of the retreat was "Client Retention." Tom organized the week with topics such as, "Who are our clients?" "Where have they gone?" "Who is left?" and "What can we do to improve?" Sprinkled throughout the retreat were questions such as, "Have we lost touch with our customers?" "Is the market changing?" "Is the competition getting stiffer?" and "What do we do next?"

Tom, Bill, Ed, and Holley spent the first retreat day discussing who their clients and customers were and defining their size, their purchase history, the length of experience, and order frequency with Allegheny. Tom brought historical files and documents to show lists of customers. They had a mix of dealer business spread out over several continents with concentrations in certain regions. They also had clients who ordered directly from the factory. However, these were usually one-time orders. The company sought orders from wherever they could, from as many channels as possible. They accepted business from all doors and in all directions. Perhaps, they thought, they should focus their sales initiatives and explore the discipline of structured market review procedures—maybe hire an industry marketing expert.

Scratching the Surface

The executive staff decided that they needed to look at the information contained in their client files. After some discussion with computer systems consultants and systems integrators, Tom recognized that he was just scratching the surface in his client database mining techniques, not really understanding the market and its dimensions. A wealth of information lay buried in their manually kept historical records, which could shed light on their possible future success. Further digging was necessary.

Analysis of Purchase Histories

The retreat team discovered during the process of sales analysis that their data analysis techniques were not able to answer all their questions. They often found themselves saying, "If only we had this computerized, we could answer these questions." They did find, however, that over a 10-year stretch, a certain segment of their dealer base always remained steady despite regional or national economic cycles. Further, they confirmed reasons why most of their profits came from a specific type of dealer in select locations.

Where Did the Business Go?

The retreat team investigated which dealers and sales disappeared in the current economic downturn. Why had many of their dealers stopped doing business with the company? The answer seemed to be that inadequate service and lack of attention drove them to do business with competitors. Buying patterns may have had an effect. "Do these dealers talk together and switch together?" they asked themselves.

The team discovered that patterns existed in certain regions. For example, when a large dealer in an area switched to another vendor, the other smaller local dealers also switched. There was some communication among these dealers that was occurring outside of the realm of Allegheny Steam Fittings.

The Problem—Too Much Data and Not Enough Information

After much work creating a manually tabulated review of their accounts, the team recognized that they had created a one-time solution. Future analysis had to be done more quickly and more frequently. Also, as a result of accumulating this information about dealer behavior, the team recognized that if they computerized the account demographic information, they would be able to make a more sophisticated analysis. They found themselves talking about the dream computer and the ideal marketing analysis system. They concluded that computers had to be introduced into the marketing and sales plan.

The Solution—A Computer and Sales and Marketing Software

To accomplish the automation task, the team decided to use microcomputers (personal computers) rather than minicomputer or mainframe technology. This would make the information accessible to everyone and allow for the use of portable computers in the future growth plan.

They purchased a 386 PC with a 200 megabyte hard disk, and they loaded all customer and client information into it. To begin with, they transferred all current account information from their IBM AS/400 minicomputer used for accounting over to the personal computer. The software review criteria consisted of features such as single-user or networking option, integrated database and word processing, sales and marketing focus, and sales support features. After a review of all sales and marketing database software, they purchased a network version of Sales Ally software, from Scherrer Resources, Inc., for this sales and marketing task. Then they created more specific fields in the database for tracking information that would be valuable in database analysis. They tracked the open date—the first date of contact with the account. They tracked the last order date and a host of other interesting facts such as the annual order amount, the product most frequently ordered, the size of dealer or customer by revenue, the number of employees, and the SIC code.

Tom began his focus by renewing business relationships with his current customers and cloning his best customers by identifying businesses that matched the profile of his most successful dealers. He also wanted to identify those that purchased in both good times and bad. As this process unfolded, Tom inspired his sales representatives to improve their service. He created monthly bonuses for service goals as measured in Sales Ally by the number of calls, actions, or meetings.

Focus on Success and Abandon Failures

The business plan required some structure—a focus for future efforts. To develop and expand new business, Tom came up with a database sorting method that identified the characteristics of his successful accounts. Then he reviewed the current slow accounts that had matching characteristics. With Sales Ally, it was easy to ferret them out. He focused on resellers doing $1,000 or more in business per month and at least $10,000 per year in their primary products. He realized that these accounts were his targets for the next 12 months and helped his sales representatives focus on this attack plan.

The Need To Eliminate Drag

From the retreat findings, the marketing team described what accounts were not ideal and developed criteria for the sales reps to use to eliminate these accounts from further marketing and sales efforts. This would prevent the reps from working with smaller accounts that were draining their time and foster a surge of efforts on those that were identified as future prime accounts. The accounts considered undesirable were tagged in the Sales Ally database with a "D-6" flag and a zero rating. D-6 was a code word for deep six, a term meaning to drop the account if possible. Code words were developed so that customers would not be offended in the event their records were read in the field.

The Rep Attack Plan

To give the sales reps the power to multiply their sales efforts, each would need to be outfitted with a notebook-sized personal computer. Research was conducted among current hardware suppliers, and proposals were solicited. The objective was for each representative to access his or her newly organized and ranked accounts on an easy-to-use and inexpensive notebook computer. The separate databases would be updated and refreshed on a quarterly basis using manual disk uploading and importing methods.

After much analysis, the company president, Bill Somers, signed the purchase order for 100 notebook computers: one for each sales representative. These notebook computers were received two weeks later, loaded with DOS and the application software Sales Ally. Then Sales Ally was filled with all the previous customer information. A computer introduction meeting was held at the next quarterly sales meeting, and a two-day training seminar was conducted. The sales reps were briefed on the strategic plan of database marketing and specifically on the objectives of increasing current customer service, revitalizing the appropriate slow accounts, and de-emphasizing those that had little potential. Another initiative introduced was the concept of cross-selling—selling additional goods to existing accounts.

Cross-Selling with Portable Computers

Cross-selling is the process of identifying current customers who have ordered certain products and selling them another product that fits their need. Crossing a steam pressure gauge line of products with a temperature gauge line of products was the first test case conducted by the Allegheny Steam Fittings sales representatives. Their second cross-sell initiative focused on selling service contracts to dealers and customers who had more than 100 employees.

The Sales Ally database helped tailor programs and special offers to attract customers to add other products to their line of steam boiler component offerings. Sales Ally was able to quickly sort the demographic information the reps needed by identifying all customers who had 100 or more employees, who used steam fittings, and who had purchased one or more pressure gauges in the past five years. This was a powerful database marketing technique. The sales reps automatically faxed a cover letter of the service offering and followed up with a telephone call to identify interest. Following this call, appointments were scheduled, and proposals were written. Proposal acceptance and product purchase usually occurred within 30 days. The sales cycle became much shorter; in some instances, it was cut in half.

Within the year, additional cross-over business from these accounts led to $1 million in additional revenue. Shorter sales cycles resulted in more frequent business from the same customers and diminished the amount of time sales representatives spent romancing accounts. In short, sales efficiency was increased.

Fax Your Way to Better Service

Along the way, the company installed fax/modem boards in their desktop personal computers. They began using the Sales Ally fax mailing technique to spread information about orders and new product features and pricing. With one merge command, Sales Ally was able to announce a new sales initiative to selected dealers and customers using the mailmerge command. The dealers received the fax overnight, and orders came pouring in the next business morning. To Tom's delight, this method became so successful that he had to install fax/modems on the portable notebook computers—the sales representatives demanded it!

Ed Brown, VP manufacturing, was caught off-guard by the rapid order process resulting from fax announcements. He quickly learned that he needed two weeks advance warning anytime a fax-merge announcement would occur. He developed a better response plan and now is prepared for order surges.

A Long-Term Sales and Marketing Plan

At the request of the president, the marketing department delivered a list of functions they would perform on an ongoing basis. These new functions were outgrowths of their discoveries of database mining and the use of portable computers in the hands of field sales representatives.

1. Define and prioritize the market with more precision.
2. Segment their customers by contribution and profit, by considering products sold, historical buying patterns, life-time value or longevity, and geographic location.
3. Reestablish stronger contact with ideal customers.

4. Create incentives according to marketing goals and not sales revenue. (For example, pay commissions to bolster the marketing plan, not for bringing in yet another small account.)
5. Use the information from the database as a way to approach the marketing plan, not vice versa.
6. Utilize notebook computers and their databases as a competitive advantage for the sales representatives in the field.

Improving Reporting

Collecting all this information into Sales Ally has no benefit unless it improves a company's understanding of its success. As a result of using the Sales Ally custom report creation feature, Allegheny Steam Fittings was able to provide improved order reports and customer profile reports. It was able to tell which orders came from what market sector or geographic location. It enabled sales managers to focus their attention on accounts that were under-performing based on the market and demographic information tracked by Sales Ally.

Summary of Results

As a result of implementing a comprehensive marketing database, Allegheny Steam Fittings has been able to develop a quick-response lead distribution program. Sales Ally software helped them to segment, profile, score, and rank prospective new accounts. It also assisted in distributing these prequalified leads to the field force for follow-up.

Further, it cut selling costs due to shortened sales cycles and elimination of misdirected selling efforts. It improved the process of handling customer complaints, opened cross-selling opportunities, and tailored marketing and sales communications. Best of all, sales commissions increased and morale improved—the ship was back in action.

The End Result

Allegheny Steam Fittings is now earning an improved profit despite a soft economy. They recognize that new computer technology helps them find, record, track, and compare accounts and gives them a competitive tool for sales success. Through the use of a powerful computer marketing database, they have become better able to implement strategic management techniques.

■ ■ ■

19

Sales Ally— An Introductory Manual

Introduction

This chapter contains an explanation of the essential features required to get up and running with Sales Ally. A complete Sales Ally reference manual containing technical advice, tutorials, hints, and advice on its use and information on new program features (such as faxing capabilities, enhanced contact records, etc.) can be obtained with program updates from Scherrer Resources, Inc., 215-836-1830.

This chapter is divided into sections. Each section is the next logical step from the preceding one. After you have read this chapter and have completed the series of small exercises, you will be a competent user of Sales Ally. You will notice that you are a much more productive individual and a member of a more effective team.

Conventions

You interact with Sales Ally by using the keys of your keyboard. You do not need a mouse.

Throughout the sections, we will tell you to use the keyboard. The two types of keyboard entries are typing text (i.e., names, addresses, numbers, etc.), and pressing specific keys (F3, 9, Enter, Shift, PgDn, etc.). If we want you to type text, we write the request as follows:

....type the phone number in the phone field....

If we want you to press specific keys, we write it as follows:

....then press F3....

or

....then press ENTER

When we write "press Alt-F3" we want you to hold down the Alt key and press the F3 key.

About Sales Ally

In this section, we will explain in general what a database is and in particular what Sales Ally is and can do. Computer application programs are categorized into a number of generic groups, e.g. spreadsheets, word processors, and desktop publishers. Sales Ally is one of the family called database management systems. A database is a collection of records. Each record consists of a number of fields. These fields contain information particular to one customer, e.g. names, phone numbers, account numbers, sales history, last date visited, etc. Nearly all companies and organizations have a database. The database is usually contained within the Rolodex, office day book, diary, customer files, and various bits and pieces of paper spread around the desk and office. This can become disorganized. Pieces of paper, memos for returning calls, and so on are often lost.

Sales Ally is an automated state-of-the-art database management system. Sales Ally can operate on either a single or a twin station or on a local area network platform. You maneuver your way through Sales Ally by using the function keys F1 through F10. As you press each key, another screen or menu layer appears with a new set of options assigned to the F1 through F10 keys. The layers can sometimes be eight keystrokes deep (see Figure 19.1).

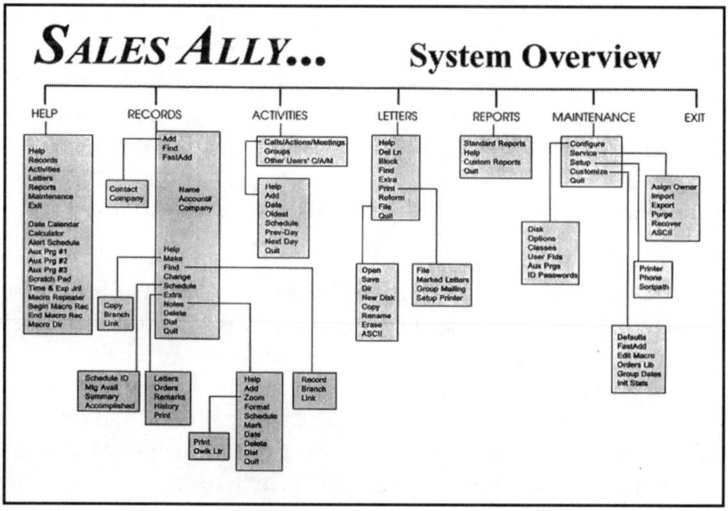

Figure 19.1 The Sales Ally menu tree

Sales Ally stores company and contact information in separate records and provides fast retrieval by name, account number, or company name. The maximum number of records is only limited by the size of your hard disk. If more than one sales person will be using the system, separate database files can be allocated to individual users. A security system ensures that each user's database is isolated from other users. The automated diary feature ensures that you never forget a call, a meeting, or any other scheduled item. The following is a list of the major features of Sales Ally.

1. *User-Defined Fields.* The 10 fields for contact records can be used to further identify a particular record. User-defined fields are useful when sorting and gathering records into groups for a particular action.

2. *Flags, Classes, Rating, and Status.* These four additional fields can be added to specific records and used later in the sort process. The Classes field supplies 26 letter-identifying possibilities. The Rating field allows numbers from 1 to 99. The data you enter into these four fields and the user-defined fields depend upon your particular business function.

3. *Contact/Company Branching and Linking.* If you have more than one contact within a company, they can all be linked to that company's record. This facilitates an easier search when you know only the company name. If there are subdivisions of companies within a major organization, the smaller companies can be linked to the major organization. Within this branched structure, contacts can be linked to companies, allowing you to find contacts easily.

4. *Integral Word Processor.* A full-featured word processor incorporates both form and custom letters. Its facilities include a spell checker and a thesaurus. Individual records or groups can be marked as receivers of a particular letter. All letters are saved in the letters file. A Quick Letter facility is provided within a contact's record. As soon as you finish your telephone call with a contact, you can write and print a short letter while the information is still fresh.

5. *Mailmerge.* Sales Ally can create the secondary merge files required by either WordPerfect or MS Word.

6. *Invoice.* Figures can be entered directly into Sales Ally. The total of sales amounts are automatically calculated. Invoices are printed directly from within Sales Ally. An invoice history is saved in a file for each record.

7. *Sorting.* A very powerful feature of Sales Ally is its capability to sort through the complete database to identify and group together records based on specific criteria. The sort criteria can be ZIP code, date, address, user field data, flags, classes, etc. You can select the customers who are in the state of Pennsylvania with a particular ZIP code or within a range of ZIP codes, who are plumbers, and who are drivers of imported cars. The more thought you invest into the user fields, Flags, Classes, and Rating fields, the more complex and useful your sorts can be.

8. *Sales Management.* For management use, a sales forecast and call statistics facility is available. The database manager can monitor the activities of the individual database users.

9. *Data Importing.* If you have a file of potential customers on disk, this file can be imported into the database as an ASCII file. Most word processors, spreadsheet programs, and database programs can export your data into this universal conversion format. If required, you must convert the file structure prior to import. During import, duplicate records can be identified. Records can also be exported to disk.

10. *Auto Dialing.* If you have a modem, you can use automatic dialing. Once you have accessed the record, you simply press the F9 key and either pick up the receiver or use a headset. The program will prompt you to answer the question, "Did you contact the person?" and all calls are logged in a history file.

11. *Notes.* The Scratch Pad, Remarks, and Scripts are three facilities for accessing written information. Scratch Pad and Remarks are pop-up screens, and their contents are linked to the record being used. The Script function is common to all records. This can contain telemarketing scripts, etc.

12. *Calendar/Calculator/Alarm.* By pressing Ctrl-F1, you call a pop-up calendar, a handy tool for specifying the dates of future return calls, etc. Another pop-up tool is the calculator (Ctrl-F2). The alert reminder (Ctrl-F3) is an alarm system that reminds you to do specific tasks during the day. You enter the time and description of each task. When the time arrives, a small caption appears on the screen, and a beep sounds. You can jot down miscellaneous jobs to do, remind the boss to call someone, or remind yourself to call the garage to check if the car is fixed. Tasks are organized in time order regardless of the entry order.

13. *Macros.* The macro facility is a simple system that automates the repetitive operation of a sequence of keystrokes.

14. *Help Screens.* A help system is available throughout Sales Ally. The help system is a pop-up text screen that is context sensitive, i.e., the help text refers to your current action.

This list of features is not exhaustive, but it should give you a good idea of the versatility of Sales Ally. Now, let's load the program.

Program Loading and Setup

In this section, we will identify the hardware requirements, explain how to install the program, and provide information on how to set up your printer and modem.

The hardware requirements are as follows:

- IBM XT, AT, PS/2, or compatible computer
- DOS 2.0 or higher for single-users; DOS 3.1 or higher for network or Twin Station Sales Ally
- 384K RAM
- A hard disk drive. A database of 1,500 records will require 2.5 megabytes of your hard disk.

Installing the Program

After you have turned on your computer and have arrived at the DOS (Disk Operating System) A: or C: prompt, follow these steps:

1. Insert disk #1 into drive A.

   Type A: and then press Enter.

   At the A:> prompt, type install and then press Enter. If the screen is difficult to read, terminate the installation by pressing F10 and start the installation process again by typing the command Install M. "M" is a parameter necessary when a monochrome monitor is attached to a color/graphics adapter.

   As the loading of each disk is completed, a message appears on the screen prompting you to insert each of the other disks.

2. When the installation is complete, a message may say `reboot the computer`. If so, proceed as follows:

   A) Remove the last program disk from the A: drive.

   B) Press and hold down Ctrl, then Alt, then Del (press all three keys simultaneously).

3. At C:>, type CD\SA3 and then press Enter.

4. To run Sales Ally, type SA and then press Enter.

   You will now be looking at the Main Menu screen. If you choose not to continue this exercise, press F10 and type Y to answer the question prompt. When you want to restart this exercise, carry out steps 3 and 4. Steps 3 and 4 are the normal way to start Sales Ally.

Printer Setup

We shall now move on to the process of setting up your printer and modem. If you do not have a printer, do not worry; Sales Ally is a valuable tool even without a printer. Indeed, in its telemarketing role, it needs no printer to function effectively. There are two printer setup procedures: one for the Letter Writer function and one for the other program functions (e.g., print records, notes, and Quick Letters). At this stage, we will lead you through the process with little explanation as we want to get on to the more interesting task of using Sales Ally. If you encounter any problems, press F10 repeatedly until you return to the Main Menu screen. You cannot damage the program by doing so. A more detailed explanation of the setup procedures is contained within the "Maintenance" section.

Before we proceed with the setup, look at your printer to ascertain the brand name, the type, and the connection port. There are essentially two types of printers: the noisy dot matrix/daisy wheel printers and the quiet laser printers. The connection port is either a parallel or serial port. If you are not certain which type of port your printer uses, check your printer manual. Both serial and parallel modes have numerically listed port options. Selecting port one for either serial or parallel is generally correct. During the setup, you need to tell Sales Ally what type of printer you have. We shall explain the setup procedure as a sequence of logical keystrokes. You only need follow them.

Having just loaded the program, you should now be looking at the Main Menu screen, identifiable by the small caption in the top right side of the screen. If you are not at the Main Menu, press F10 until you see the caption that says Main Menu.

Next, press F8 to access the Program Maintenance section. Press F6 to select the printer option and press F2 for printer. Figure 19.2 illustrates the Printer Selection options.

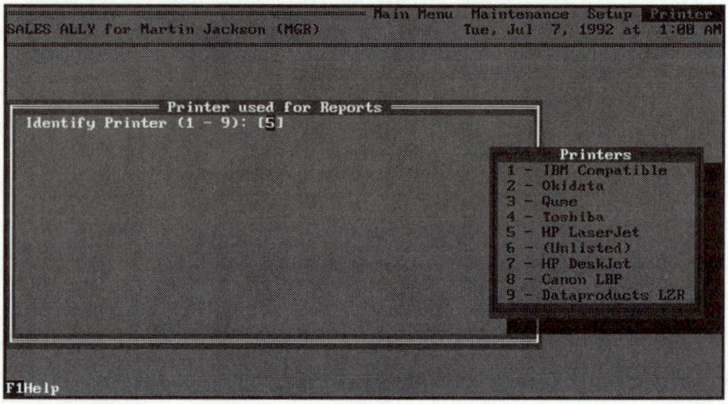

Figure 19.2 Printer selection options

You now select the type of printer that you have. Do not worry if you do not have a printer from the list. If it is a Hewlett Packard LaserJet variety, select LaserJet; if it is a dot matrix, select either the same brand name as yours or, failing that, select the IBM printer. Many printers use the same commands as the IBM.

Type the number that corresponds to your printer and press Enter. Next, you must specify the computer port to which your printer is connected: either parallel #1 or #2 or serial #1 or #2. Make the appropriate selection and press Enter. If you are not certain, try parallel #1 first; it is the most common.

The series of questions that follow relate to the page and label setup of your printer. You will notice a comment box that advises you to accept these settings as the default. Therefore, press Enter to accept these defaults and to get to the end of the printer setup screen. If you have selected the wrong printer or port, do not worry; you can change the settings later. We shall use the printer in the next section, so you will have an opportunity to test your choice.

Now press F10 to revert to the Main Menu. Leave the screen in its present position; you will need it for the next section.

The printer setup procedure for the Letter Writer function is similar, and we will explain it as part of the Letter Writer section.

Using Sales Ally

In this section, we will explain the basics of getting started by entering records, amending records, reviewing the record fields, producing printed copies of records and Quick Letters, and sorting records into groups.

Entering Records

This is the time to gather all those dog-eared business cards, small bits of paper, memo notes, and your office Rolodex. Prior to entering your records, we will proceed with a short tutorial where we will enter five records. There are two types of records within Sales Ally, a Contact record and a Company record, the main difference being that a Company record has no personal name field. At the Main Menu screen, press F2 to select Records. Press F2 to Add to the database, and press F2 a third time to add a Contact Record. Your screen should now look like Figure 19.3.

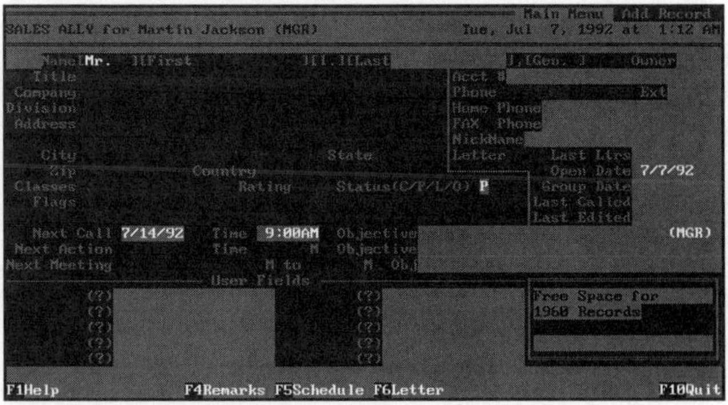

Figure 19.3 A contact record screen

A rectangular block indicating the position of the cursor is now in the salutation field (top left of screen). There is a default of Mr. in the field. Press Enter or the down-arrow key to move the cursor to the next field. Type Tom in the first name field and press Enter. You move around the record fields by pressing Enter or the down-arrow key. Move to the surname field and type Jones. A surname entry is the minimum amount of data required to enter a Contact record in the database. If all you have is a telephone number, enter the surname AAAA as a temporary place holder and call the number to get the name to add later.

Using the down-arrow key, complete the normal address fields and move the cursor to the phone field. Type 999-999-9999 and then press Enter or the down-arrow key. Phone numbers require a hyphen to separate the area code. Note that the record started with a date in the open date field. Now let's look at the classes, flags, rating, and user fields. Classes are one criterion used to sort your database. Manufacturers and distributors are examples of classes. Classes are identified by the letters A–Z, and you will define the labels for these letter codes in the Maintenance section of Sales Ally. You can assign up to 12 of the 26 classes to any one record. Classes are added to a record by choosing the command to edit a record and moving the cursor to the Classes field.

Flags are also used to sort your database on more specific product criteria than classes. Flags can be defined as a more detailed specification to be used as a handle on that record. For example, you might have a customer who is interested in widgets and gadgets. You could list this customer's flags as WIDGETS, GADGETS. The flags field will accept words, acronyms, or single-character codes. Flags can be entered in any order, but they must be separated with a comma.

Is this prospect *hot*? Do you want to call him or her first before other customers ? The Rating field is used to designate the "temperature," or importance, of a customer. Choose a number from 1 to 99 with 99 being a "hottest" customer.

You can define 10 user fields in Contact records and 10 more in Company records. One of the maintenance functions allows the you to label, type, and specify the range of each field. Although the maximum length of a user field is 15 characters, you can customize the database in many ways for personal use.

User field types include numeric, date, string, and a variation of the string called table. By identifying a field type, you can validate data as it is entered. Thus, if the user were to create a date-type field, anything entered into this field in a record would be validated as a date before being accepted. String type data are any arrangement of letters, numbers, or special characters; thus, validation cannot be performed on entered data.

The table-type user field accepts a string that is searched for in a predefined table. If the string is not found, the user is alerted and given the opportunity to correct the entry or add it to the table. If, when making an entry, you would rather pick a string from a table rather than type it, you can press F2 Pick to pop up a window containing all strings previously added to the table. You then can highlight the appropriate string using the arrow keys and press Enter to paste the selected item into the user field. User fields are assigned by type from within the Maintenance Section.

Now let's investigate the calls, actions, meetings, or activities fields. You will notice that a date and time is entered in the calls box. This was entered as a default number of days after the current date, and the default date can be changed in the "Maintenance" section. These fields are important to the diary feature of Sales Ally. One option when entering records is the F5 Schedule that is used to record events for future action. Press F5, and the cursor is in the date box of the call field. Notice that the keying options at the bottom of the screen have changed. There are two methods for entering a new date; one is to enter the number of days into the future to schedule the event, and the second is to enter a specific date in the format shown. We shall do the former by typing 14 and pressing Enter. Notice a new date 14 days from today is displayed. The time field is entered in the normal format. Move the cursor to the objective field. This field is best used for small notes to explain the diary entry. Type "Has he paid invoice? Perhaps 14 days is too short a period to expect payment. Let's figure a better date." Press Ctrl-F1. The pop-up screen is the Sales Ally calendar. It features step forward or backward by month and indicates the days of the week. Pick a working date 30 days from the invoice date by which time you would expect payment. Press Esc to remove the calendar pop-up. Move the cursor back to the date field of the calls box, and type the new date for payment. Thus, you have completed a diary entry. We will explain the operation of the calls, actions, meetings field later in this section. Press F10 to exit the calls, actions, meetings field.

We have now completed the essential fields in a contact record. Press F10 and you will be prompted to input notes. Type Y in answer to the prompt. You are now in the Note Pad. All notes are saved with the contact record and are available for reference when the record is used. Notes can be assigned dates. From the keystroke options, Press F3, and the Note Pad expands to fill the screen and allow more information to be read. Press F10 and you will exit the Note Pad and this record. The Jones record is still shown on the screen, but now the Main Menu function key options are available.

We now have one Contact record in the database.

Entering a Company Record

Let's enter a Company record and use some other features. Press F2 Records, press F2 Add, and press F3 Company. A blank Company record screen (see Figure 19.4) will be present with the cursor in the first field to be entered.

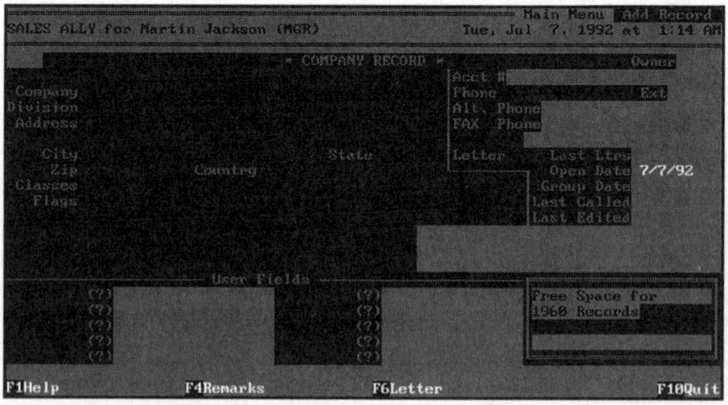

Figure 19.4 A company record

Enter in the appropriate fields the details of your company. When prompted to input notes, reply N for no. Press F10 to exit the record. You should be back with the Main Menu keying options.

We will now exercise the find feature of Sales Ally by accessing the Contact record of Mr. Jones. From the Main Menu options, press F2 Records, press F3 Find, and press F2 Contact. You are prompted to input the contact's name. By default, although changeable in the "Maintenance" section, the input name should be the contact's surname. At the prompt, type Jones and press Enter. Mr. Jones' record is displayed. Notice that the available function key options have changed from those displayed during the Add process. Input an address for Mr. Jones by pressing F4 to change the contents of the record. Move the cursor through the address fields and enter a suitable address. Assuming that you have met Tom Jones and that you are on first name terms, fill in the nickname field with Tom. Press F10 when you have completed the field entries.

Although you have pressed the F10 key to exit the record change option, you are still in Mr. Jones' record and your keying options are not yet back to the Main Menu options. (You would press F10 one more time to get back to the Main Menu.) We will write Mr. Jones a Quick Letter. Press F7 to access the Note Pad. Press F3 Zoom, press F9 Quick Letter. Notice that the date, address, and Tom's name appear on the letter. Had we not assigned Tom as the nickname, the salutation would have appeared as Mr. Jones. Write a letter of inquiry regarding the probability of his purchasing some of your products. The letter must be short—only 46 lines are available. For longer letters, you can use the Letter Writer feature discussed later. Now press F7, and the Quick Letter will be printed. The letter is saved and is available each time Tom's record is accessed.

Copying Common Data to New Records

To illustrate the copy feature, exit Tom's record by pressing the F10 key the required number of times. From the Main Menu, press F2 Records, press F3 Find, and press F4 Company. Enter the company's name at the name prompt (only a partial name is required to start the search), and your company's record will be displayed. Press F2 Make, press F2 Copy, and answer the prompt by typing Y. You now have two options, a contact or company copy. Choose contact by typing Y. A Contact record with the surname NoName will now be made. Press F4 to change this record and enter the name Harry Jackson. Move the cursor down the fields to the Classes field. Type A to give Mr. Jackson the class of end user. This copy feature can save time.

Let's create another record to illustrate some other features by copying Harry Jackson's record. Give the record the name of Dick Martinson. In Dick's Classes field, type B. In Dick's Rating field, type 99—Dick is a hot prospect! Use the up-arrow key to reverse your way through the record. Because Dick is such a hot prospect, we will send him a letter from within the Letter Writer. When you have finished inputing his rating, press F10 to revert to the record menu keystrokes. Press F6 Extra and F2 Letter. Type D for a listing of the Letter Writer file directory. Select letter 02 and press Enter. Notice that the digit 2 appears in the letters field.

To summarize, you can now enter both Contact and Company records manually. You can copy and change them. You have written and printed a Quick Letter and made Notes. Along the way, you will notice that many of the keying options have not been explained. This chapter is only an introduction to the power of Sales Ally.

Printing Labels

To print labels, use the Reports feature of Sales Ally. The Reports feature enables you to select a group of records by specific criteria. To assist us in this section, we deliberately placed certain criteria (e.g., Classes field entries) in the four records you entered.

The process of printing labels or using any of the other features is to select the desired output form—labels, reports, mailmerge, etc. Select the records by specific criteria and carry out the action—print, mailmerge, etc. The Report feature is initiated by pressing F6 from the Main Menu options. See Figure 19.5 for an illustration of the Reports screen.

Use the arrow keys to position the cursor over the Name and Address selection options. Press Enter and press F6 Display Options. (See Figure 19.6 for an illustration of selection criteria.)

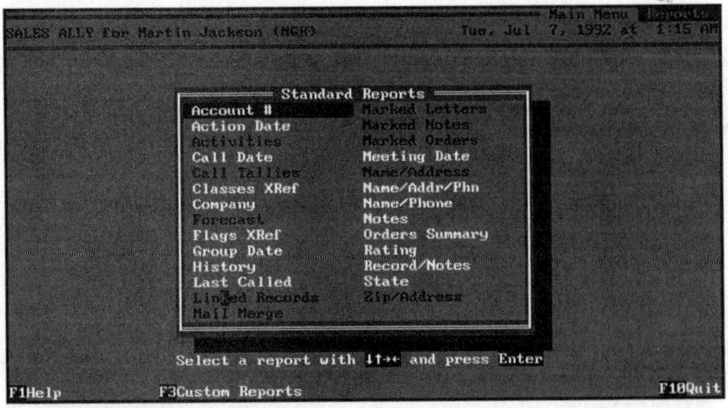

Figure 19.5 Reports Selection menu

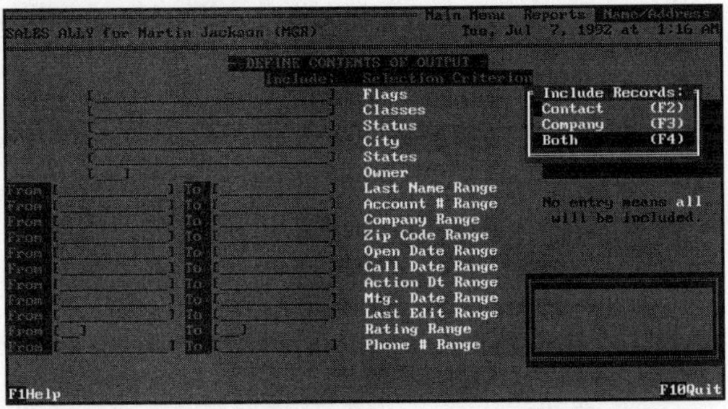

Figure 19.6 Reports Display options

The first decision to make is whether you want to select records based on Contact, Company, or both types of records. Press F2 to select the default Contact. Now enter the detailed selection criteria. We have four records, but only three are Contact type, and only one has the unique Class of A (an end user).

By pressing the Enter key, you will move the cursor down to the Classes box. If you do not enter anything into a particular box, you are instructing the system to include all possible entries for that field. In the Classes box, type A. Press PgDn to finish entering the selection criteria.

You will be prompted to apply a group date to these records. If you are going to use these selected records again, it is advisable to assign a group date, as you can use that date for later recalling the same records. For our example, type N for no. If you have a lightning fast machine, the selection will complete by now. Failing that, the screen will indicate that it is sorting. The amount of time to complete the sort depends on the speed of your machine, the size of your database, and the number of criteria you have entered. A 286-based machine may take 35 seconds to work its way through 1,500 records, and a 486-based machine would certainly be quicker.

When the sort is completed, a list of selected records will appear on the screen with a message to use the spacebar to scroll through the list.

Press F7 to print the output. You will be prompted `Do you want labels?` Type Y, and labels will spew from your printer.

Macros

Many folks skip the Macro section of the most commonly used application programs. The thought of learning a complex computer programming language is too much to bear. This is not so with Sales Ally.

As you now know, Sales Ally operates by pressing the function keys in sequences. When your database is up and running, the same key sequences are being used over and over again, for example, marking a group of records for a letter. This repetitive chore can be greatly facilitated by automating the keystrokes.

In Sales Ally, macros consist of a series of consecutive keystrokes that are saved in a file. These saved keystrokes can be played back by pressing the assigned hot key. Imagine the chore of changing the Call Date to three days hence in 50 records. The keystroke sequence for one record is F5, Ins, 3, Enter, F10, F10, down arrow. At seven keystrokes a record, that makes 350 keystrokes and much boredom. Within Sales Ally, the seven keystrokes can be reduced to two by recording them as a macro and assigning a two-key hot key such as Alt-F. Sales Ally further increases efficiency by enabling a macro to be repeated a specified number of times.

Sales Ally comes with a number of commonly used macros. All macros are stored in a library, which may be reviewed at any time (except when the Letter Writer is in use) by pressing Alt-F1.

Macros are recorded in real time—that is, you put yourself at the start position of the keystroke sequence. Press Alt-F9 to turn on the macro recorder. At the prompt, assign a hot key and start the key sequence. When you have completed the key sequence, Press Alt-F10 to turn the macro recorder off. Finally, you will be prompted to give the macro a short explanatory title.

If you want to automatically repeat the operation of a specific macro, press Ctrl-F9. You will be asked which macro you want to execute and how many times you want to repeat its operation.

Maintenance

The Maintenance section is accessed from the Main Menu by pressing the F8 key. The Maintenance section contains the Configuration, Service, Setup, and Customize functions. Generally speaking, these facilities make global changes to the Sales Ally system, your database, and other user databases. Let's look at a couple of important features on the Maintenance menu.

Backup

Like the majority of application programs, backup is not an integrated facility in Sales Ally. Nevertheless, backing up is very important. On at least a weekly basis, be sure to carry out the following task:

1. Insert a floppy disk in your A drive.
2. Exit any application program and go to the DOS prompt C:.
3. Type Backup C:\SA3*.BTR A:. (The spaces between commands are important.)

   All your important data files will be backed up in files that have a .BTR extension.
4. Select F2. Configure.

The Configure option (F2) facilitates such tasks as changing the screen colors, assigning passwords, and defining the three auxiliary programs that can be invoked by pressing the keys Ctrl-F4, Ctrl-F5, or Ctrl-F6. The paths and filenames of the assigned auxiliary programs are entered by pressing the F6 key. Programs initiated by batch file (files with .BAT extensions) cannot be invoked in this fashion.

The definition of the User Fields of both Company and Contact records can be changed, added to, or deleted from within the Configure section (F2). The assignment of Classes to their associated text is defined here.

Service

The Service section (F4) contains the facilities for importing and exporting records, assigning a collection of records to a particular user, or purging (deleting) the notes or history for selected records. The important recover feature will assist you if your record files become damaged.

Setup

We have discussed previously the printer setup facility in the Setup F6 section. You may also set up a printer within Letter Writer. If you are planning on using the automatic dialing feature of Sales Ally, you will need to set up your modem. To set up your modem, tell Sales Ally what type of modem you have installed and to which port it is connected. If you are unsure if your modem is Hayes compatible, try it first. If you do not know to which com port your modem is connected, pick port one; chances are you will be right. To test your modem setup, access a record and press F9. Listen for the dialing and ringing tones. If you do not hear anything, try com port two. If you still hear nothing, return to com port one and try the other modem selections. If all else fails, read your modem instruction manual.

Customizing Features

You may select Fast Add fields here. Selecting the minimum number of fields that the cursor will access during Fast Add eases the burden of imputing records manually. The defaults facility enables you to preset some field entries, e.g., the City, the ZIP, or the Salutation can be preset. If you are loading many records, all of which are in the state of Utah, presetting UT will save time.

The command to remove a group date from a selected group of records will save even more time than a macro doing the same job. An important management feature called Phone Statistics is initialized within the Customize section, and Custom Reports can be generated detailing the telephone activity of individual users.

Letter Writer

The Sales Ally integrated word processor performs a multitude of letter writing tasks. You can compose new letters, amend old ones, send individual or group mailings, and merge record information to produce personalized letters. All customary word processing features are available by using the function keys. An optional spell checker and thesaurus are available.

Prior to learning about Letter Writer, let's set up the printer. The Letter Writer has additional printer options such as proportional fonts. Press F5 to access the Letter Writer. You will notice that there is a time delay while Sales Ally swaps out, and the Letter Writer screen appears. This swapping out of the program prevents the macro facility from working in the Letter Writer. You should now have a screen that looks like Figure 19.7.

Selecting a Printer

You have only three function key options. First, we will look at option F6 Print. From the pop-up menu, move the cursor to Printer Setup and press Enter. Select your printer or the one most compatible to it. If you have added a font cartridge, be sure to select the correct cartridge.

Under the name of your printer is a list of printer options. For now, press Enter to accept each of these options as defaults. Press Esc to exit this setup menu.

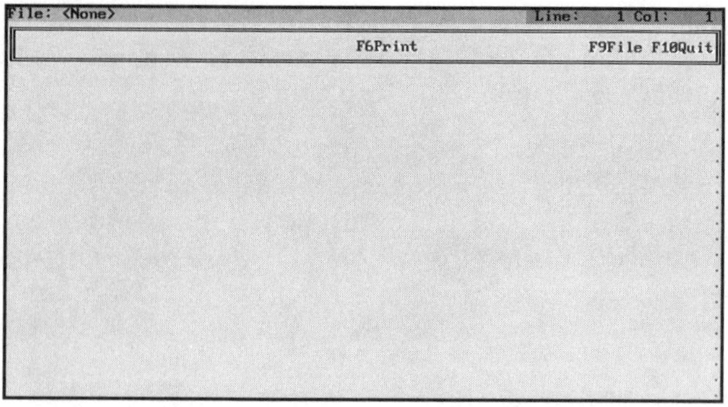

Figure 19.7 The Letter Writing screen

Printing a Letter

Press F6 to recall the printer menu. Place the cursor over File and press Enter. You will be prompted for a letter file number. Type 02 as a sample and press Enter. Press Enter again to accept the default of one copy. Letter number 02 will now print. Look to see what has printed. If the general look and feel is good, then you have a reasonable printer setup. If you printer has the capability, you can change the pitch and character size by pressing F1 Help.

Although you can send single letters, you will generally use the Letter Writer to do group mailings. In a manner similar to the mailmerge function of other word processors, the finished letter is the product of two inputs. One input is your form letter that contains the merge codes, and the other input is the database file of names and addresses of the recipients. The Letter Writer merges these two inputs together by substituting the names, addresses, and other fields for the merge codes. You can view the possible merge codes by pressing F1 and selecting Merge.

■ ■ ■

Hardware and Software Vendors

Product	Price	Company	Address	City	State	ZIP	Phone Number
ACT!	$395	Contact Software International	1625 W. Crosby Road #132	Carrollton	TX	75006	214-418-1866
Agenda	$99	Lotus Development Corp.	55 Cambridge Parkway	Cambridge	MA	02142	617-577-8500
Aldus Persuasion	$495	Aldus Corporation	411 First Avenue South	Seattle	WA	98104	800-685-3539
Alpha 4	$495	Alpha Software, Corp.	One North Avenue	Burlington	MA	08103	800-451-1018
BitFax/SR	$79	BIT Software Inc.	830 Hillview Court, Suite 160	Milpitas	CA	95035	408-263-2197
BRS Information Services	n/a	BRS Search Service	800 Westpark Drive	McLean	VA	22102	800-955-0906
Calendar Creator Plus	$80	Power Up! Corporation	2929 Campus Drive	San Mateo	CA	94403	415-345-5900
CompuServe	n/a	CompuServe	P.O. Box 20212	Columbus	OH	43220	800-848-8199
CrossTalk	$99	Digital Communications Associates	1000 Alderman Drive	Alpharetta	GA	30202	404-442-4000
Current	$395	IBM Desktop Software	472 Wheelers Farms Road	Milford	CT	06460	800-426-7699
Day Timer	$20	Daytimers Inc.	1 Daytimer Plaza	Allentown	PA	18195	800-556-5430
dBASE IV	$795	Borland International	1800 Green Hills Road	Scotts Valley	CA	95067	408-438-5300
Dialog Information Services	n/a	Dialog Information Services	3460 Hillview Avenue	Palo Alto	CA	94304	800-334-2564
Excel	$495	MicroSoft Corporation	One MicroSoft Way	Redmond	WA	98073	206-882-8080
Freelance Graph./ Windows	$495	Lotus Development Corp.	55 Cambridge Parkway	Cambridge	MA	02142	617-577-8500
GrandView	$295	Symantec Corporation	10201 Torre Avenue	Cupertino	CA	95014	408-253-9600
Harvard Graphics	$595	Software Publishing Corporation	3165 Kifer Road	Santa Clara	CA	95051	408-986-8000
HotLine Two	$60	General Information Inc.	11715 N Creek Pkway, Ste 106	Bothell	WA	98011	206-483-4555
HP ScanJet IIp	$1,295	Hewlett-Packard	19310 Pruneridge Avenue	Cupertino	CA	95014	800-752-9000

Product	Price	Company	Address	City	State	ZIP	Phone Number
Internal Modems, Generic	n/a	Holmes Microsystems, Inc.	2620 South 900 West	Salt Lake City	UT	84119	801-975-9929
Konexx	n/a	Unlimited Systems	5555 Magnatron Blvd, Suite J	San Diego	CA	92111	800-275-6354
Lists On Disk	$750	American Business Information	5711 South 86th Circle	Omaha	NE	68127	402-593-4565
Lotus 1-2-3	$495	Lotus Development Corporation	55 Cambridge Parkway	Cambridge	MA	02142	617-577-8500
MCI Fax	n/a	MCI Mail	111 19th Street, NW	Washington	DC	20036	800-444-6245
National Database	$195	Arc Tangent	121 Gray Avenue	Santa Monica	CA	93101	805-965-7277
NEC Intersect CD Drives	n/a	NEC Technologies, Inc.	1255 Michael Drive	Wood Dale	IL	60191	800-632-4636
OmniPage Direct	$595	Caere Corporation	100 Cooper Street	Los Gatos	CA	95030	408-395-7000
OmniPage Professional	$995	Caere Corporation	100 Cooper Street	Los Gatos	CA	95030	408-395-7000
On The Go Fax	n/a	Ibis Software, Inc.	625 Second Street, Suite 308	San Francisco	CA	94107	415-546-1917
On Time	$130	Campbell Services, Inc.	21700 N.W. Highway, #1070	Southfield	MI	48075	313-559-5955
Pack Rat	$395	Polaris Software	1820 Escondito Blvd. #102	Escondito	CA	92025	800-338-5943
Paradox	$795	Borland International	1800 Green Hills Road	Scotts Valley	CA	95067	408-438-5300
Professional Mail	$695	Arc Tangent	121 Gray Avenue	Santa Monica	CA	93101	805-965-7277
PT-10L	n/a	Panasonic	One Panasonic Way 2D9	Secaucus	NJ	07094	201-348-7000
QA-1050	n/a	Sharp Electronics Corp.	Sharp Plaza	Mahwah	NJ	07430	201-529-9500
Quattro Pro	$495	Borland International	1800 Green Hills Road	Scotts Valley	CA	95067	408-438-5300

Product	Price	Company	Address	City	State	ZIP	Phone Number
R:BASE	$795	Microrim	15395 S.E. 30th Place	Bellevue	WA	98007	206-649-9500
Sales Ally	$395	Scherrer Resources, Inc.	8100 Cherokee Street	Philadelphia	PA	19118	215-836-1830
SmartOffice	n/a	EZ Data	533 S. Atlantic Blvd.	Monterey Park	CA	91754	800-777-9188
TeleMagic	$495	Remote Control International	5928 Pascal Ct.	Carlsbad	CA	92008	800-992-9952
Windows	$150	MicroSoft Corporation	One MicroSoft Way	Redmond	WA	98073	206-882-8080
WinFax/Pro	$119	Delrina Technology Inc.	6830 Via Del Oro, #240	San Jose	CA	95119	800-268-6082
WordPerfect Office	$189	WordPerfect Corporation	1555 N. Technology Way	Orem	UT	84057	800-321-3253
Zip++	$195	Arc Tangent	121 Gray Avenue	Santa Monica	CA	93101	805-965-7277

Index

G-H

I-L

O

P

Q

R

S

T

Sales Ally Disk Contents

Enclosed is Sales Ally, Version 3.10, for your use in learning the ideas presented in this book. As an example of a portable selling tool, it will provide you with practical experience in installing and using integrated sales support software. An explanation of the application for Sales Ally is presented in Chapter 13, and in Chapter 19 you will find the Sales Ally introductory manual.

After using this learning tool, you may want to obtain further information from the software developer by writing or calling:

Scherrer Resources, Inc.
8200-2 Flourtown Avenue
Philadelphia, PA 19118
(215) 836-1830 (voice)
(215) 836-1804 (fax)

Also available from this vendor are fee-based telephone support, user manuals, and version updates.

DISK REPLACEMENT ORDER FORM

In the event that the disk bound in to this book is defective,Prentice Hall Computer Publishing will send you a replacement disk free of charge.

Please fill out the information below and return this card to the address listed below with your original disk. Please print clearly.

BOOK TITLE_______________ ISBN_______

NAME_______________ PHONE_______

COMPANY_______________ TITLE_______

ADDRESS_______________

CITY_______________

STATE_______

ZIP_______

Prentice Hall Computer Publishing
11711 North College Ave
Carmel, IN 46032
ATTN: Customer Service Department.

LIMITED WARRANTY REGISTRATION CARD

In order to preserve your rights as provided in the limited warranty, this card must be on file with PHCP within thirty days of purchase.

Please fill in the information requested:

BOOK TITLE_______________ ISBN_______

NAME_______________ PHONE NUMBER(___)_______

ADDRESS_______________ CITY_______ STATE_____ ZIP_____

COMPUTER BRAND & MODEL_______________ DOS VERSION_______ MEMORY_____K

Where did you purchase this product?

DEALER NAME?_______________ PHONE NUMBER(___)_______

ADDRESS_______________ CITY_______ STATE_____ ZIP_____

PURCHASE DATE_______ PURCHASE PRICE_______

How did you learn about this product? (Check as many as applicable.)

STORE DISPLAY___ SALESPERSON___ MAGAZINE ARTICLE___ ADVERTISEMENT___ OTHER (Please explain)_______

How long have you owned or used this computer?

LESS THAN 30 DAYS___ LESS THAN 6 MONTHS___ 6 MONTHS TO A YEAR___ OVER 1 YEAR___

What is your primary use for the computer?

BUSINESS___ PERSONAL___ EDUCATION___ OTHER (Please explain)_______

Where is your computer located?

HOME___ OFFICE___ SCHOOL___ OTHER (Please explain)_______

PUT
FIRST
CLASS
STAMP
HERE

Prentice Hall Computer Publishing
11711 N. College Avenue
Carmel, IN 46032

Attn: Order Department

Mail-Order Selling Made Easier

By John Kremer

A step-by-step guide to organizing and carrying out a successful direct marketing program which will explain how to get more inquiries from your ads, and more orders from your inquiries.

Publisher's Price $19.95 **(59450)**
Member's Price $16.95 Bonus Price $9.98

How Much Is Enough?
Getting the Most from Your Advertising Dollars

By John Phillip Jones

Solid strategies for more effectively budgeting, planning, and implementing advertising. 288pp. 2bc.

Publisher's Price $35.80 **(53706)**
Member's Price $26.95 Bonus Price $17.90

The Executive Program®

Newbridge Book Clubs, Delran, New Jersey 08370

How To Earn Bonus Books:

- For each regular selection you purchase and pay for, you earn a Bonus Credit. Books with member prices over $19.95 earn two (or more) credits. You earn your first Bonus Credit by paying for your Introductory Package.
- When you have earned four Bonus Credits, you may order any book offered in The Business Bookshelf brochure at the low Bonus Price (50% off the Publisher's Price).
- To order a Bonus Book, list your selection on the reply card. Be sure to circle the B to indicate a Bonus Book Selection.
- Books purchased at the Bonus Price do not earn Bonus Credits.
- Please note that the number of Bonus Credits you've earned is shown on your reply card. Since the reply cards are printed in advance of their mailing, they do not always reflect credits earned by your most recent payments or credits subtracted due to a recent Bonus Book purchase.

How To Order Books:

If you wish to purchase the Main Selection, do nothing and it will be shipped to you automatically on the date shown on your order card. If you wish us to ship the Main Selection **immediately**, check the appropriate box on your order card. If you wish to order an Alternate, Special, or Business Bookshelf Selection, or no book at all, simply indicate your decision on the enclosed order card and return it to us by the date specified.

How To Find the Correct Book Price:

For each book in this Business Bookshelf brochure, you'll find three prices. The first price shown is the Publisher's Price. The second is the Member's Price. The third, the Bonus Price, is the price of the book when ordered as a Bonus Selection. You are entitled to make a Bonus Selection after you have earned four Bonus Credits.

How To Read the Abbreviations in This Brochure:

SC indicates a softcover book. SB indicates a book that is spiral-bound. *bc* stands for bonus credit(s). If a book is not specified SC or SB, you may assume it to be hardcover.

Your Membership Number:

Please include your membership number on all checks and correspondence.

Change of Address:

If you plan to move, please give us as much advance notice as possible—two months' notice is perfect.

Take any 2 books FREE

When you get a friend to join The Executive Program®

★ ★ ★ To be Filled in by the Present Member ★ ★ ★

Please send me – absolutely **FREE** – the 2 books indicated below upon acceptance of my friend's application. (NOTE: The publishers' price for the books may not exceed $60.00 and your selection is limited to books from this brochure. If you prefer, you may take one more expensive book worth up to $60.00.)

Book Code Number / Publisher's Price

1. ____________________ ____________________
2. ____________________ ____________________

Total publishers' price (Total cannot exceed $60.00) ____________________

Name ____________________ Account # ____________________

Address ____________________ City ____________________ State ____________ Zip ____________

PLEASE NOTE: If you have not made a payment to the club, you may be asked to provide additional credit information before your friend's application is accepted.

★ ★ ★ To be Filled in by the New Member ★ ★ ★

Please accept my application for trial membership and send me the three volumes indicated, billing me only $1.00 each, plus shipping and handling. I agree to purchase at least 3 additional Selections or Alternates over the next 12 months. Savings range up to 30% and occasionally more. My membership is cancelable anytime after I buy these three additional books. A shipping and handling charge is added to all shipments.

No-Risk Guarantee: If I am not satisfied – for any reason – I may return my introductory books within 10 days, and I will owe nothing.

(Books purchased for professional purposes may be a tax deductible expense. Offer good in Continental U.S. and Canada only. Prices slightly higher in Canada.)

3 books for only $1.00 each

(Note: Selections are limited to the books from this Business Bookshelf brochure. If you prefer, you may take only two expensive books, or even one $75.00 volume.)

Book Code Number / Publisher's Price

1. ____________________ ____________________
2. ____________________ ____________________
3. ____________________ ____________________

Total publishers' price (Total cannot exceed $75.00) ____________________

Name ____________________

Address ____________________

City ____________________ State ____________________ Zip ____________

★ ★ ★ How The Club Operates ★ ★ ★

At 3-4 week intervals (15 times a year) you will receive The Executive Program® News describing the upcoming Main and Alternate Selections together with a dated reply card. In addition, up to three times a year, you may receive offers of Special Selections which will be made available to a group of select members. If you want the Main Selection, do nothing and it will be sent automatically. If you prefer another selection, or no book at all, simply indicate your choice on the card and return it by the date specified. You will have at least 10 days to decide. If, because of late delivery of the News, you should receive a book you do not want, we guarantee return postage.

The Executive Program®

MGM

Newbridge Book Clubs, Dept. MGM, Delran, N.J. 08370

3-896/893
D-896/1193

Comes with a 50-minute audiotape!

"The success characteristics discussed in TOUGH SELLING FOR TOUGH TIMES are a must for those people who want to make it in the 1990's and beyond."
—Ken Blanchard, coauthor of *The One-Minute Manager*

TOUGH SELLING FOR TOUGH TIMES

By Murray Raphel and Neil Raphel

"If you buy only one business book this year, make it TOUGH SELLING FOR TOUGH TIMES."
—Jerry Reitman, Executive VP, Leo Burnett Advertising

It was the best of times, it was the worst of times. . . . In their new book/audiotape package, **TOUGH SELLING FOR TOUGH TIMES,** Murray and Neil Raphel demonstrate how your business can prosper even when times are tough.

Tough times can mean an economic recession. It can mean a competitor opening a new store down the block. Or a bank refusing to extend a loan. Or the loss of a key employee. Or a flood destroying your inventory. . . .

This book is about "tough" selling steps that you can use to achieve business success—proven steps that businesspeople have used to overcome adversity. Each chapter focuses on a different characteristic of business success—and each chapter contains stories, quotes, interviews, anecdotes, and advice. Taken altogether, **TOUGH SELLING FOR TOUGH TIMES** is a program for success that you can apply today in your business. **TOUGH SELLING FOR TOUGH TIMES** shows you:

- **How to find out what your customers really want—and give it to them**
- **The 10 characteristics of top salespeople**
- **The five reasons people do *not* buy (and how to overcome them)**
- **And more**

TOUGH SELLING FOR TOUGH TIMES is full of promotional ideas, customer service secrets, tips on customer retention, and infectious enthusiasm!

"The lessons readers find in the book are timeless, as effective for the tough times as for the not-so-tough ones." ***—Memphis Business Journal***

"Get a copy of TOUGH SELLING FOR TOUGH TIMES! . . . It's a book for anyone who wants to be outstanding in sales of any type." —Syd Ascher syndicated columnist

About the Authors

MURRAY RAPHEL is president of Raphel Marketing, Atlantic City, New Jersey. He travels over 200,000 miles a year and speaks internationally on marketing. He has written several books, including *Mind Your Own Business*.

NEIL RAPHEL is an attorney, author, and vice president of Raphel Marketing.

Save $10.00!

- **197 pages, with a 50-minute audiotape**
- **6" x 9"**
- **Published by Raphel Publishing**

(84461)

Publisher's Price $29.90

Member's Price $19.90

Earns one bonus credit toward the four required for your next Bonus Book

3-116